I Inc.

CAREER PLANNING AND PERSONAL ENTREPRENEURSHIP

SECOND EDITION

D0921211

by **MIKE CALLAHAN**

UNIVERSITY OF MICHIGAN–DEARBORN

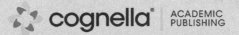

cognella® | ACADEMIC PUBLISHING

Bassim Hamadeh, CEO and Publisher
Kassie Graves, Director of Acquisitions and Sales
Jamie Giganti, Senior Managing Editor
Miguel Macias, Senior Graphic Designer
Carrie Montoya, Manager, Revisions and Author Care
Natalie Lakosil, Licensing Manager
Kaela Martin, Associate Editor
Abbey Hastings, Associate Production Editor
Rachel Singer, Interior Designer

Cover image copyright © Depositphotos/urostomic.

Printed in the United States of America

ISBN: 978-1-5165-1495-3 (pbk) / 978-1-5165-1496-0 (br)

I am dedicating this book to my nephew, Dr. Joseph Laythe.

Joey left us way too early, but his memory will continue to live on in many ways. He was a gifted historian and taught his students in a way that I will continue to try to emulate.

He always made it about the students and how he could help them in their quest for knowledge. We had the privilege of setting up an endowed scholarship in his name, and he wanted to be sure that the beneficiaries would be single students who were raising a child while going to college.

He continues to inspire me, and I am so fortunate to have known him as a close relative, a friend and an advisor. His legacy will live on in so many different ways.

CONTENTS

SECTION 1: SETTING THE STAGE

CHAPTER 1: CONTEXT FOR SUCCESS   15

SECTION 2: EXPLORING YOUR PASSION

SECTION 4: TELLING YOUR STORY

CHAPTER 9: DEVELOPING WRITTEN TOOLS 175

ACKNOWLEDGMENTS

Support for this book comes from many sources, but the first, and most important, comes from my wife, Sandy. She consistently encouraged me to keep working and never give up. I would not have completed the first edition had it not been for her support. That encouragement has continued through writing the second edition, and she continues to provide me with insight and valuable perspective that I know will bring value to my students.

I was also blessed to have the opportunity to further develop and apply these concepts in my role at the University of Michigan–Dearborn. I am thankful for the opportunity and ongoing support I have received from staff and faculty in the development of these ideas. Specifically I would like to thank Pam Morris for her support in applying the I Inc. concepts to her counselling sessions with students and also to Tuere Wheeler and Farah Harb who both teach sections of our Career Planning Course and have given me valuable input into how to better teach the class but also how we can include more valuable content in the book. I also want to thank Joan Martin, our College of Business Librarian, for the insight and content she has provided me that will help our students be much more informed when they do go in for that important interview.

And lastly, I would be remiss if I did not mention the support and encouragement I have received from our son, Wade, our daughter, Stacy, and their families, as well as my sister, Susan, and other family members and friends. It truly is wonderful to have the support of so many different people in this endeavor.

My sincere thanks to everyone who helped me make this a reality.

ENDORSEMENTS

I Inc. takes career planning and development to the next level. It not only gives you the tools to succeed; it shows you how to use those tools effectively. In today's job market, you need more than a fancy cover letter and a professional résumé; you need the key to success, and *I Inc.* offers that. It's not full of big words and complicated concepts.

I Inc. is an easy read, and with a little effort, it can be easily implemented. Coming out of a fourteen-year career, I felt ill prepared for today's job market; having the opportunity to read *I Inc.* has changed that. Through *I Inc.*, Mike Callahan shares his vast knowledge of career planning and development, and as one of his former students, I am forever grateful.

—**Rochelle Rutledge,** Senior, University of Michigan–Dearborn

"Why are you the best fit for this position? What are your strengths?" These may seem like easy questions, but they're a lot more difficult to respond to. This book will help you develop and sell your personal brand through identifying your strengths and interests, creating a career plan, and connecting what you have to offer with what the market is seeking.

—**Farah Harb,** Coordinator, Ford Fund Education Program; Former Assistant Director, Career Planning and Placement Office, School of Business, Wayne State University

I Inc. is a tremendous foundational tool that shows how to build a career on your own terms. This book showcases the necessary entrepreneurial building blocks to form traits every professional has to have while crafting individual self-branding. Mike helps illustrate the principals of identifying what you're truly passionate about and following your personal "why" in a career, rather than blindly chasing money.

—**Justin Hnatio,** Business Development Manager, Biznet Digital

The book *I Inc.* by Mike Callahan widely contributed to my success in landing an internship with a Big 4 public accounting firm. This book not only helped me develop a long-term career plan for myself, but also served as a vital part of helping me understand my personal brand. Before reading this book, I was unsure of what qualities I would use to market myself during networking events, interviews, and so forth. However, this book helped me discover what qualities make me unique and would contribute to my success during professional events. In addition, I learned how to write a pristine resume and how to become a competitive, successful interviewer.

Thanks to everything this book has taught me, I was able to be an extremely memorable candidate during the interview process and receive internship offers from every firm that I applied to for an audit internship. After accepting an internship offer, I even heard from my peers that their interviewer brought me up in conversation and shared my unique qualities. I also applied the concepts from this book during my internship and ended up receiving a job offer at the end of my internship. I would highly recommend this book to help individuals succeed in their career goals and I hope you will find it just as amazing and supportive as I did.

—**Kelly L. Fitch,** Accounting Student, Senior,
University of Michigan–Dearborn

I Inc. has opened my eyes to a different side of professional development and how to properly activate my very own "triangle of success." The professional world can be very bare at times, but Mike Callahan has created a book that stimulates the desire to switch gears from neutral to drive and navigate the pathway to become the driver of your own car(eer).

—**Jacqueline Beazley,** Marketing Student, Junior,
University of Michigan–Dearborn

FOREWORD

by MICHAEL PALMER

CEO and Founder, Hire INsite

H aving spent the better part of my career focused on helping organizations attract, identify, hire, and engage talent, writing a foreword for
this book—a book that so clearly articulates a logical and practical approach
to the management of your career—I am left with an incredible sense of
empowerment. I have proudly known Mike Callahan for many years and have
learned a great deal about my craft from him. He has had a profound impact
on my career.

In I Incorporated, Mike reveals an anecdote that was undoubtedly a significant
contributor to the direction his life and career would end up taking. I met Mike
while we worked for a large Fortune 100 organization; he was entirely devoted and
loyal to the company and had been with this company for many, many years. Yet
with a directional change from our CEO, he found himself working within a company that had a fundamentally different set of guiding principles and challenged
his personal ethics. This change, though it may have been subtle, was a catalyst
that changed Mike's career direction and arguably was one of the best things that
happened to him professionally.

From this experience, I remember having a sudden realization that the fate of
my career was in my hands, no one else's. There is no greater feeling than being the
master of your own domain. The empowerment is astonishing! I adopted Mike's
concepts wholeheartedly. The only one who is accountable to your career is you.

When I left school to begin my career, it was common for those a generation
ahead to have worked in one career and frequently with one employer their entire
working lives. Today the average tenure at a company for professionals is three
years. Many of today's midcareer adults are in a second or third career. The ability

to see, track, and grab the "brass ring" is not only a desired skill set, it is required. The entrepreneurial mind-set that is required for success is the foundation of today's working world.

This book does an excellent job of arming you with the tools you need to stand out from the crowd, whether you are looking for your first job, your tenth job, or are setting out to build up your own business. The concepts in this book are not only practical, they are essential if you are going to be successful in your career.

As someone who has interviewed thousands of candidates for many different roles, the difference between those who embrace personal empowerment versus those who are at the mercy of their circumstances is absolutely incredible. Owning your future, staking your claim, and driving toward your future will not only set you apart from the competition, it will put you on an entirely different trajectory. Remember this is your career. Own it.

I have had many incredible successes in my career and have had many opportunities. I do firmly believe that we make our own luck. As an entrepreneur myself, I know that Mike's lessons are a guidebook to success. Just add hard work.

SECOND EDITION UPDATES:

I INC., CAREER PLANNING AND PERSONAL ENTREPRENEURSHIP

We have had the benefit of using this book for the past two years in our Career Planning and Development Course and had had the opportunity to use the material with over 700 students in helping them plan their careers. We have three professors teaching the subject and each week we review the material, develop our plans for the coming week and add any new content that we feel is valuable for our students. In addition, we have received critical feedback from other faculty members outside of our university regarding how to make the book more valuable to their students and have also received feedback from students about what they like and what they would want improved.

As a result of both the feedback received and our experiences, we have decided to make several changes to the content in this edition.

We have changed the sequence of the chapters to make them flow more logically along with the actual development of someone's personal career plan. We have added additional content in all of the chapters that reflects what we have learned over the past two years and how we can present the material to our students in a more meaningful way. We have added a sizable amount of content to help students do more detailed research of potential employers. We have added an entirely new chapter on the idea of a "Sweet Spot" and how best to bring your brand, value and opportunity together in a meaningful way. We have also added a new section to each chapter called "Additional Resources" that can help both graduate and undergraduate students find other tools to help them in their specific situations.

We are excited about the second edition and have attempted to include both feedback from other professionals and students but also insight from actually using the book to teach the class. We feel that we have been able to both capture new content and update existing content to make it an even more valuable tool. We hope you share this excitement as you read the book, explore some of the additional resources and apply some of the concepts that are suggested in each chapter.

SECTION 1.

SETTING the STAGE

INTRODUCTION

Here is a news flash for you! The traditional way of looking for a job by posting your resume and waiting for someone to contact you is dead! In fact, it never really did work very well, but with the widespread adoption of the internet and job boards, it is truly dead. Recruiters are overwhelmed with the number of resumes they receive, so to survive they have installed software routines that scan resumes looking for key words. If you think that this is a good way for you to be represented in the selection process, you are going to be disappointed with the results.

The positive thing about all this change is that there is a new paradigm to respond to the rampant changes in the economy. It is this new approach, which we have borrowed from the experiences of successful entrepreneurs, to help you create new opportunities. However, in order to pursue the new opportunities, you will be required to develop a new way of thinking.

In this section, we introduce you to a new framework: how to begin to change your mind-set, how to take advantage of the opportunities provided in the free market, and how to embrace a guiding context that will serve you for many years to come.

BEGIN THE JOURNEY

WHY IS THIS TOPIC IMPORTANT?

Do you ever wonder why some people have outstanding career opportunities no matter what they do, while most of us struggle just to find a job and keep one? What is it about these people? They are not smarter, stronger, or better looking than the rest of us, and they are not graduates from better schools. What do they possess?

That is what we will explore in this book. What are the key differentiators that help some people excel in their career pursuits while others struggle, flounder, and even sometimes fail?

When you look at the current literature in career planning, you find numerous books about taking control of your career, developing a powerful elevator speech, learning how to brand yourself, paying attention to the details of your resume and cover letter, and even mastering the nuances of successful interviewing. The problem with all these approaches is that they are simply approaches. They are the tools and techniques that some people use to excel while others just do not quite make it happen. Here is the clue. It is not about the tools. It is about how the tools are used and the context within which they are used.

WHO IS THIS BOOK INTENDED TO SERVE?

Actually, the audience for this book is anyone who wants to engage in today's job market. It might be someone who is finishing college, someone who is in midcareer and looking to change his or her direction, or even someone who has retired and is looking to begin a new career. The concepts will serve everyone who is engaged in an active career-strategy development.

You notice I say "career-strategy development" and not "a job search." For too many people, a job search is equated with developing a resume and then mailing it to as many people as possible, hoping that someone gives you a job. That is not what this book is about. What it is about is helping people decide to take control of their career quest and not rely on someone else to make the decisions. After all, it is about you, and your life and your career aspirations. You are the only one who truly knows what those are, so you must be completely in control of the career quest. When you send an unsolicited resume to a potential employer, you are not in control. When you wait around for your company to make a decision about the fate of your job or your department, you are not in control. And when you retire from your current job and are wondering what is next, you are not in control.

College undergraduate students can use it to help them begin to develop a strategy to pursue their careers. Too many students are graduating and going into jobs that they could have done with a high school education. If you are in this boat, then do not let that happen to you. There are ample opportunities out there, but you need to learn to pursue them in a powerful and valuable way.

Also, you might be a graduate student with several years of experience and wondering if this is the right book for you to be using. It will definitely serve your needs also. Since you have experience, you will be even better able to capitalize on those experiences and use them to help shape the value proposition that you want to bring to the market.

The bottom line is that this book is aimed at any individual who want to be in control of their career quest and are willing to do the required work, take the risks and accept the uncertainty of being accountable for their lives and their careers, and benefit from the outcomes.

This journey is not for those who are willing to let someone else decide the fate of their career but is definitely for those who want to take that control and pursue a strategy that will help them attain the career opportunities that are consistent with what they are capable of achieving.

CONTEXT BEFORE CONTENT

So, you might want to ask how someone goes about taking control of their career. Why are some people able to do so easily, while others struggle to make it work in their lives? Part of the answer lies in the idea of being clear about the context of the job search before you focus on the content and is the fundamental tenet of this book. If you do not have the context created first, you will be randomly chasing every new scheme that comes up promising a good job and a prosperous future.

Be careful! Do not jump into the content before you have given the opportunity to fully develop the context.

Developing a resume is an example of content. Writing a cover letter is another form of content. Even building a LinkedIn profile is content. All these things, along with many other tools, are absolutely necessary in the career quest, but if you start with them, you are condemning yourself to continuing to repeat the past. If you try to write your resume as the first step in your quest, you wind up talking about what you have done instead of how it can help you promote your unique abilities and target the kind of opportunity that you want to pursue.

I hope that you give yourself permission to focus on the context first, and then let the content flow out of that context. If you do, the probability of success is going to be much greater.

When we talk about context in this sense, we are talking about you being an entrepreneur of your own career and, as a result, being much better at assessing and marketing your own personal abilities, choosing the environment in which you want to work, and ultimately the effectively using the required tools to help you let people know just how special you truly are. Once the context is clearly established, then the intended results can be achieved.

You Must Have Context Before You Have Content!

A wise man and dear friend, Dr. Peter Koestenbaum, told me once that you must have context before you can have content. The context for that conversation was a strategic planning meeting with a group of executives at a company where I once worked. It was evident that as a team, we needed to get clear about how we wanted to operate before we spent any time talking about what we wanted to do. That concept is true in business relationships, but it is also profoundly true in career planning and development. You must have the proper context before you can develop the content.

Too often, people jump into the process prematurely. They pick up a book on resumes, branding, or interviewing (that is, content items) and do not spend enough time thinking about the context. They pursue the perfect resume as though it were the magic elixir that will guarantee them a job, or they jump into

LinkedIn and try to connect with everyone they can find. Remember: You must have context before you can have content!

We will develop a context in this book that has universal appeal. It will be easily understood and actually is quite recognizable, but in a slightly different application. Although it has been successfully developed in a somewhat different setting, it does have a strong track record for success.

Does that sound interesting? Well, the context that we are describing is that of entrepreneurship. Essentially, it is about treating an employer like a client. It is about creating a framework for you to operate in that will set in motion many actions and activities that will serve your career quest. By deciding that you are an entrepreneur of your career, you take full control—and responsibility—for what happens in your career. It is yours. You own it, you are in control and are ultimately responsible for everything that happens to you in the pursuit of your career ambitions.

ENTREPRENEURSHIP DEFINED

According to *Merriam-Webster's Collegiate Dictionary,* the definition of an entrepreneur is simple. It is defined as the "one who organizes, manages, and assumes the risks of a business or enterprise."

Why do I think there is a clear link between pursuing your career aspirations and pursuing a business venture? When you are pursuing your career aspirations, you must organize your approach, manage all the factors that can come into play, and be prepared to assume the risks associated with the career quest. And that sounds like the definition of an entrepreneur.

All of this implies that you must have some skin in the game. You must be wedded to the outcome and have the passion and drive for success an entrepreneur has, and that drive has got to be obvious.

In my current role I have the opportunity to meet with many students who are struggling to find a job opportunity. Unfortunately, their approach is often somewhat passive and even noncommittal at times. They believe that the way to find a job is to have a strong resume and then get that resume in front of a hiring manager. In his book *What Color Is Your Parachute?,* Richard N. Bolles claims that the hit rate for using this approach is 5 percent to 10 percent, and yet most people rely on it as their main career strategy.

If an entrepreneur took a similar route, he or she would create a product description based on past accomplishments, produce some flyers, and then hope someone would bite. That approach may work occasionally, but in order to be successful on an ongoing basis, an entrepreneur must do a comprehensive scan of the market, develop a plan to penetrate that market, develop a valuable product and/or service to serve the market, and then follow through with all the challenges and obstacles that come up. In order for an entrepreneur to be successful, it is mandatory he or she follow this approach, and for an individual pursuing his or her career interests, the same thing holds true.

SUCCESSFUL ENTREPRENEURSHIP VENTURES

There are many examples of successful entrepreneurship ventures. Some are very high profile such as Apple Inc. or Microsoft, but many are small, local businesses that are able to thrive in a competitive environment.

If we are going to borrow a page from the world of entrepreneurship to guide our career pursuits, we need to learn a little about what are the characteristics of a successful business venture. Jan King in her article "The Top 10 Reasons Businesses Succeed" has done a great job of identifying most of the key elements that are required in today's competitive market. The key point to understand is that these are required for a business to be successful and they are just as important for you to be successful in the pursuit of your career.

Here is the list of the top 10 things that any business will need in order to prosper:

1. The experience and skills of the top managers are strong and versatile.
2. The key members have high levels of persistence and resourcefulness.
3. They produce a product or service that is a cut above the competition.
4. Their service enables the customer to buy their product.
5. They can create buzz about the product or service.

6. They know how to manage the customer's perceived value of the product or service.
7. They continue to develop new products and services.
8. They control their expenses.
9. They treat everyone fairly.
10. They know how to locate their business in the most beneficial location.
11. They have a product/service mix that can weather the ups and downs of the market.

Take a critical look at this list, and see if you can relate to how you could pursue some of these objectives as an individual pursuing your own career. Are you persistent and resourceful? Do you know how to make your product (you) a cut above the competition? Do you have a sense of how you might be able to create buzz about you and the value you bring to a company? This is not an easy task but if you are able to replicate these requirements in your own personal quest, you will truly be able to have a successful career.

Now, the harsh reality is that even if we use the entrepreneurship example to guide us, it will not guarantee success. In fact, many entrepreneurial ventures do fail in the first few years of existence. It seems that if we wanted to use another model to help with the career planning, we would choose something with a stronger track record than being an entrepreneur.

However, it is in the successes and the failures of entrepreneurs that we can learn a lesson about how to make our career-acceleration plan more successful. We looked at what makes a business a success, now let's look at the flip side to see some potential reasons for the failure of start-up business venture. There are some that float to the top fairly quickly. They are:

1. Inadequate market research
2. Inadequate financial backing
3. Inadequate product/service knowledge
4. Insufficient drive to make it through the tough times

Throughout the book, we will be talking more about how you can capitalize on those desired traits while overcoming many of these obstacles in your own career quest. Suffice it to say that they are real and drawn from actual experience, and the approach I am proposing can be fraught with challenges and obstacles. However, the benefit you can receive will greatly outweigh the cost, and to be fully empowered in your career pursuits it is worth tackling these challenges and taking full control of your career.

HOW A CAREER CAN GET OFF-TRACK

One more thing to consider before we wrap up this chapter is to ask the question: "How can a career get off-track"? There are obviously lots of things that can happen in one's life to derail a career but there are some specifically tied to this approach that deserve mention.

Specifically, it can happen when you lose sight of what got you there in the first place. You may have built a solid value proposition, have a competitive product and are able to promote it effectively, but then the world changes. A new factor enters the workforce. It might be technology, or less expensive labor, or even a change in customer's perceptions, but the change comes, and if you are not constantly reviewing this list and confirming that you are remaining competitive, you can become obsolete. Never believe that what got you to your position will continue to serve you. I want you to learn how to use these principles and then continue to reuse them for the rest of your professional life.

LEARN TO THINK LIKE AN ENTREPRENEUR

Before we go any further, I want to be clear about the concept of thinking like an entrepreneur. It does not mean that you need to be an entrepreneur and go start your own business. In fact, that is not the most desirable path for many of you, and this book is not about starting and running a successful business.

However, it is about taking the concepts that help people start and run businesses and learning how to apply them in your personal career quest.

Bottom line: I challenge you to embrace the idea that the opportunities in today's market require a new type of mind-set. That mind-set is to be more entrepreneurial in your thinking and in your approach to opportunities. Thinking like an entrepreneur will provide you with much greater control over your career destiny.

STRUCTURE OF THE BOOK

FIVE SECTIONS

It is obvious that this context has been successful in helping people launch businesses. Now you will be able to apply many of the same concepts in your personal career development, so that when you choose to apply a tool or a process, you will be operating out of a solid context that has a proven track record.

FIGURE 1.0. FIVE SECTIONS OF THE BOOK.

The book is organized along five sections. The first is all about "Setting the Stage" and introducing you to the concepts that we will be exploring. The second section is titled "Exploring Your Passion" and will help you gain a deeper understand of your personal interests, strengths and weaknesses, propensities, and even survival strategies that will come into play in your career quest. The third section shifts gears and helps you take your abilities to the market, or what we call "Discovering the Opportunities." It will help you develop an even stronger sense of who you are, where you want to work, and how can you bring value to given opportunities. We finish that section with the idea of a "Sweet Spot" where it can all come together for you, involving your brand, your value proposition and the under-served opportunities that exist. The fourth section is all about "Telling Your Story." This is where a lot of the content items come into play, but only after you have done the required preparatory work. Finally, the fifth section, titled "Making It Happen," gives you strategies to launch your career-acceleration plan and develop an approach that will serve you for many years to come.

LAYOUT FOR EACH CHAPTER

Each chapter will introduce and develop examples within the context of comparing and contrasting how you might develop a career-acceleration plan to how you might create an entrepreneurial business plan. Remember, the idea is that you want to borrow the successful strategies from the world of entrepreneurship and apply those concepts within your personal career quest. In addition to making the theoretical connection, we will also include some suggested resources that can help you understand and embrace the concepts even more fully.

As we get close to the end of each chapter, there is an "Additional Resources" section that will give you access to many other resources on the internet and in different areas that can help you with your career quest. And then, at the end of each chapter, is a section titled "Now What?" The intention of this section is to cause you to stop and think about what you just read, translate it into the new mind-set of being an entrepreneur of your career, and then identify specific actions that you can take to help improve your ability to successfully apply the concepts in your own personal career quest as well as some specific steps to take to help build your personal career plan.

I invite you to read on, and in so doing, develop a crystal clear understanding of these concepts so that you too will be able to fully take advantage of the myriad of tools and techniques available for you in the successful pursuit of your career aspirations.

REFERENCES

Merriam-Webster's Collegiate Dictionary, 11th Edition, Merriam-Webster, Inc. (July 30, 2003)

King, Jan B. *The Top 10 Reasons Businesses Succeed, http://www.streetdirectory. com*

1

Context for Success

CHANGING WORKPLACE

In case you missed it, in 2005 Thomas L. Friedman published a book titled *The World Is Flat: A Brief History of the Twenty-First Century*. He did not argue that the world was actually flat but rather argued, very effectively, that the world is becoming much smaller and opportunities are open to just about anyone who is willing to take the risk and engage in the marketplace.

He argued that everything is changing. How we work, where we work, how we compete, how we perform and are evaluated—it is all changing. Also, he made the case that competition is not just within our local areas but can come from anywhere in the world.

This change can be unsettling, but it also can be full of infinite opportunity. Those people who know how to adapt and how to operate in today's marketplace will be able not only to survive but to prosper.

Some of the more significant consequences of these changes affect us directly in our ability to compete but also in the realization that we must continuously look at what we do for a living and confirm that it has true value to our employer. There is simply way too much competition today for anyone to become complacent and rest on his or her laurels. The workplace is changing at breakneck speed, and it is imperative that individuals who want to be successful in this environment understand the value that they bring and be able to explain it again and again to those who are constantly looking for a better way to get the job done. Employers can draw from a global pool of talent, so you must be able to market your skills effectively, both in the short run and throughout your entire career.

A SOBERING STATISTIC

Pew Research Center did a survey of college graduates and asked them what they would have done differently while in college, and fully 50% said they would gain more work experience, while 30% also admitted that they should have started looking for work sooner. I have also heard it said that over 50% of recent college graduates go into a job that they could have done with a high school diploma.

Whether you look at recent surveys or just conduct your own informal research, you will come away with the understanding that it is critical for you to understand and embrace the idea that the world of work is constantly changing and you have to engage, get some experience, learn what you are good at doing and what you do not like to do, and become fully engaged in the career development process. Waiting until you are close to graduation is not a wise move and will not get you the kind of opportunity you deserve.

CAREER PLANNING NOW! DON'T WAIT UNTIL IT IS TOO LATE

Another way to think about this whole idea of career planning is to borrow another page from industry. You might want to look at the idea of pursuing a career along the same lines as a company pursues the idea of Just in Time Supply Chain Management.

We all know that we will clearly need to find a new opportunity when we graduate, but if we wait until then to start planning, we will be behind the curve in the process. In much the same way that a company needs to do a large amount of planning and preparation so that they can receive that needed part at exactly the right time, you too should be thinking about your career planning process way ahead of the time when you actually need to make the change.

Also, even if you are a graduate student and already have job, don't forget that as you go through the career planning process and think about the value that you are bringing to the job market, it will also benefit you and your current employer in ensuring that you are valuable in your current role even if you have no desire to change employers.

The bottom line is that you don't want to wait until you need the job before you start your quest. If you do so, you will be scrambling with your resume, frantically looking for someone to "hire you" and can potentially fall into a state of significant desperation.

As an alternative, take up the challenge now to begin to plan for the future in much of the same way that a company plans for its future involving just in-time inventory management. You want your career prospects to arrive "just in time" and that requires significant planning ahead of time.

WHICH CAMP ARE YOU IN? IT IS YOUR CHOICE

There seem to be two camps when it comes to personal career planning and development.

One camp is that of dependency. People in this camp are expecting some-one else to do the heavy lifting when it comes to their career strategy. They want to hire someone to write their resume. They want to rely on a place-ment agency or their college career center to find them a job. They believe that their college degree and other credentials are sufficient and that all they need to do is to get the information out there, and someone will scoop them up and pay them a nice signing bonus in addition to a comfortable salary. Their biggest problem with this approach is that these people will get very little play in the job world and spend most of their time waiting for something to happen.

And then there is the other camp. These folks are hungry. They are looking for opportunities every time they meet someone. They take personal ownership of their career quest. They own their resumes and their elevator speeches. They know the value that they can bring to an employer, and they are constantly on the lookout for opportunities. Their biggest problem is that they wind up with several potential opportunities and do not know which one to pursue. Which, by the way, is a very nice problem to have.

So which camp are you in? The first one is relatively easy, and is dependent on someone else to do most of the hard work. The second one is actually hard. It takes work and dedication, and it requires you to take a risk and put yourself out there. It is fraught with potential rejection but it also has unlimited opportunity.

They key is that it is completely up to you to choose your camp. It is not driven by your parents, or your significant other, or by your friends. It is your choice!

This has got to be one of the most significant decisions that you make in your career quest. Are you in the camp that is hoping someone will give you a job or are you in the other camp where you are totally in control of your career aspirations.

Choose wisely, it is completely in your hands.

FREE MARKET ECONOMICS

The reality we all face in pursuit of our career aspirations is this thing called the free market. This is where goods and services are exchanged for a price. What is important to remember is that while the nature of work and how it affects the individual employee are going through a major transformation, the fundamental concepts behind the free market are not changing.

The free market has been in place for a long time. It has been the creator of fortunes for many people but has also contributed to the ruin of many others. The ultimate irony is that the market can be both very cruel and infinitely rational and fair. In fact, it is totally devoid of emotion. It does not care where your parents were born, what language you speak, your religion, your age, or your gender. It only cares if you are able to bring value to it in exchange for fair compensation.

It is important to understand but also respect and embrace this concept. When we ask someone for a job, we are asking him or her to do us a favor and give us something. But if we accept that we operate within the free market and decide to bring our service into the market in exchange for a fair price, we are taking full advantage of the opportunities that the market can provide. There is a profound difference between asking someone to give you something—such as a job—and offering to provide value to someone in exchange for compensation!

HOW JOBS GET FILLED

Dick Bolles in *What Color Is Your Parachute* has done an outstanding job contrasting how jobs get filled with how people search for jobs. His argument is that a job seeker begins with their resume, then might look at some want ads, work through an agency and maybe contact some of their colleagues. They seldom work through referrals, contacts, showing up at an employer's office with the right credentials or working within the company. The reason that people do it that way is that they know how to do it. They can find a book on resumes or go to the want ads or contact an employment agency for help. They do not know how to do it any other way!

Contrast that with how jobs actually get filled. According to Bolles, hiring managers look within the company, check with their networks or respond if the right person comes along with the right credentials. They will go to agencies or the want ads and grind through a bunch of resumes if they have to, but they would rather get a solid recommendation from a colleague and go with that option.

This is what we want to help you understand in this book. We want you to learn how to operate in the world where jobs are getting filled and to differentiate yourself from the vast majority of people who still believe that the best way to get a job is to send your resume to as many potential employers as possible. In essence, we want to help you be better prepared to operate in a free market economy.

DOES THIS APPLY TO A MORE EXPERIENCED STUDENT

In the prior chapter we mentioned that this approach is good for both a newly graduated student as well as for someone with more experience. In fact, someone who has already been in the work force or has more extensive experience is going to be even better able to take advantage of the ideas in this book and use them to be more effective in working with hiring managers who are looking for talent.

By being able to leverage your current experience, you will be even better able to reach out to hiring managers, make the kinds of connections that you need and land a solid opportunity.

The key idea, regardless of your level of experience, is that you need to let go of the old way of thinking about your career as a series of resume mailings and embrace the new approach where you are contacting hiring managers and making the connection outside of the traditional job posting systems.

MY DEGREE IS: (PICK ONE)—DOES THAT DEFINE THE WORK I NEED TO PURSUE?

Something else to consider when you are deciding which companies to reach out to is to not be limited by the type of degree you have earned or are earning.

Too often, a student tries to make the direct link between their major and the specific field where they will work. The problem with that approach is that most universities focus on a broad education, as they should, and are not trade schools focusing on a specific set of skills. They are preparing students to be critical thinkers, problem solvers, communicators and leaders and the student's major is an area of focus but does not represent the entire spectrum of possibilities.

I try to encourage my students to give voice to their true passions. I want them to take the time to decide what their "super powers" truly are and then to pursue opportunities that will capitalize on those powers. When a political science student says that he or she has to go into politics or when an economics student feels that the only careers available to them are as economists, they are cutting themselves short.

Take the time to understand and give voice to your passion. Understand that employers want to know about your skills and knowledge but also about your experiences and track record as well as how you can connect and relate to others.

Understand what you are really good at doing, pursue some opportunities to sharpen those abilities and continually focus on pursuing those situations that will reward you for those abilities. Take advantage of the skills and knowledge that a given major has afforded you, but don't let it be a hindrance. Rather, let it provide you with some basic knowledge that you can then leverage into a viable career option.

The world has more opportunities than any of us can possibly imagine. Approach your personal career quest from a perspective of abundance and go for those opportunities that truly tap your potential.

Take a little time to think about and reflect on the idea that the market will reward or punish you, without emotion, based on the value you bring to it. It is as simple and elegant as that. No emotion!

People often complain that the market is cruel because it does not care what your personal needs are. In reality, it does not care that you have been working for a company for more than fifteen years, that you just had a new baby, or that your house needs significant upgrades. When people approach the market hoping someone will "give them a chance" because they need or deserve something, they are fooling themselves. In essence, they are asking an unemotional entity to be nice to them and give them an opportunity to show what they are capable of producing.

Never forget that the market is not inherently cruel. It simply does not care. It is infinitely rational and will give the best opportunity to the person who can deliver results at the lowest cost and at the highest quality.

If you forget this fact, you can easily be lulled into a false belief that the firm will take care of you. If you work for a certain company for a long time and then are suddenly fired because the company has decided that in order to remain competitive, it must outsource some of the work, it is easy to feel betrayed and bitter. After all, you have given that firm years of your life. You have been loyal, and now you feel betrayed.

If you feel this way, it is possible you failed to realize that for all that time, you were being paid a fair wage by the company. You received what you were due based on the agreement that was established when you were hired. However, if you chose to naïvely believe the company would watch out for you in the long run, and in so doing forgot to watch out for yourself, then you are the one to blame. You simply allowed yourself to get lulled into a false sense of security.

What you might have failed to realize is that you needed to keep your personal value proposition current and relevant. We will go into much more detail about the idea of a personal value proposition, but it essentially represents the value you bring to the market and ultimately to your current employer. And it is just as important when you start your career as it is fifteen to twenty years later.

I have also heard it said that a regular paycheck can be similar to crack cocaine. You get addicted to it and will do most anything to protect it—except review your current value to the marketplace and develop a plan to ensure that you are bulletproof.

I do not mean to imply that there are not managers within a given company who are concerned for your well-being and will do what they can to help you in your career quest. Managers are people too, and they do have emotions. It is just important to realize the company will collectively behave in an unemotional and rational manner, and you must accept that truth if you are going to flourish in today's economy.

However, that does not mean all is lost. In fact, even though the market appears to be cruel, it is infinitely logical and fair to those who know how to successfully operate within its constraints. If you bring the best value to the market, you will find many different opportunities! This must represent how you approach the market when you are initially looking for a position, and it is also something you must do throughout your career. Understand what the market needs and don't wait around for someone to "give you a chance."

You can do it! It can be unsettling at first and is definitely outside most people's comfort zone. The key is to embrace the concept and do a critical assessment of your current skills and track record, and then develop a plan to build the capability you need and promote yourself to the market. Then do your research so that you can better understand what the market needs. Get rid of the belief that you need someone to "give you a chance." Create a personal brand. Learn how to market yourself; if you do, you will be bulletproof.

It really is the only thing that has ever worked, and it is ingrained in the American psyche to be independent and resourceful. Take control of your career and you will never feel that you are leading the life of quiet desperation described by Thoreau.

We live in a time when psychological contracts are frequently broken between employees and companies, record numbers of students graduate from college without jobs, and our inner cities struggle simply to survive. All the while, there are jobs going unfilled in technical fields as well as in other areas where we can be competitive.

This book is about taking control of your career destiny. It is not about how to develop an award-winning resume or how to dazzle employers with the use of social media. Those are valuable tools, and we will certainly cover them in this book, but it is much more important to have a solid grasp of the context in which you are currently operating before you try to develop the content. Most of the book is focused on creating the proper context for a successful career strategy.

Tools are important, but they must be used to support the context we develop and pursue on a consistent basis.

GUIDING CONTEXT

What is this context? The idea is quite simple. Be an entrepreneur of your own career destiny and use the following graphic to help chart your course. The three dimensions, represented by the three sides of the triangle, are what employers look for in an individual.

SKILLS AND KNOWLEDGE, TRACK RECORD, AND RELATIONSHIPS

The skills and knowledge dimension represents your ability to actually do the job. Do you know what you must do in order to be successful? Furthermore, can you do it, and do it at a level of performance that will be acceptable to a given employer?

How we satisfy this dimension is constantly changing. Technology rapidly makes some skills obsolete while introducing new ways to perform work. You should always be aware of the skills and knowledge that are valued in the workplace and focus on continuing to enhance your ability to compete.

Take a look around you. Look at how other people are able to do their jobs. Look at what you are able to do. Ask yourself if you are staying current with technology. Are you learning the new processes in the workplace? Are you curious about the new skills and knowledge that are emerging? It is easy to look back and see how PCs displaced many people who were tied to mainframe computers and the associated technology.

Embrace the changes. Look at your abilities, and constantly look for ways to improve your overall skill and knowledge related not only to what you currently do, but even more importantly, to what you want to do in the future.

However, just knowing how to do the job is not enough. Recruiters want to know how you will do it—or even if you can do it in their environment. Hence, we have created the second side of the triangle, which is the track record. Having the ability is only part of it; you must be able to discuss instances when you have demonstrated the ability to perform.

Think about why so many recruiters ask for a certain number of years of experience. It is the track record dimension that they are looking for. Realize that fact, and if you do not have the experience related to what you want to be doing, figure out how to get it. You may need to do some volunteer work or even a part-time second job in order to get the experience. And do not forget, it has to be current. What you did several weeks or months ago rapidly becomes obsolete. Keep your track record current and relevant!

Lastly, there is the relationships side of the triangle. You must be able to discuss how you will fit in with the organization. What kind of values do you share with other people in the organization? It is crucial that you be able to discuss the relationships you build, both to assure the recruiter that you will fit in to their environment and to help assure yourself that it is the kind of environment where you want to work.

Building relationships takes time and effort. It is not simply about having some names in your address book. It is about making connections and nurturing those connections even when you do not need them to do something for you.

We have created repeatable processes that will help us develop these three segments. These processes are represented by the diagram in the center of the graphic in figure 1.1 and contain the key activities for you to pursue in order to develop your career-acceleration plan, much in the same way an entrepreneur would develop a viable business plan.

The major sections of the book will go into much more detail on each of these elements, but suffice it to say that you will need to consider nine unique and highly integrated processes in your career pursuit.

I have known many executives who complain that people often contact them only when they need a favor. If you are one of those people who only reach out to your contacts when you are looking for a job, then you are not nurturing a relationship. You have to be willing to go beyond your comfort zone and meet new people, and you also have to commit to taking the time to invest in the relationships, and maybe even offer to help your contacts in addition to asking them to help you. This dimension takes just as much time and effort as do the other two. They are all important and will not develop and flourish unless you give them the dedicated effort that they require.

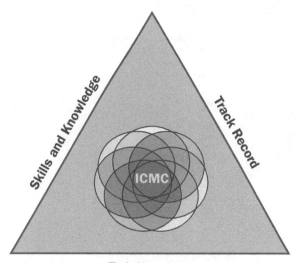

Relationships
Internship and Career Management Center

FIGURE 1.1. TRIANGLE OF SUCCESS.
Copyright © by Internship & Career Management Center, University of Michigan-Dearborn. Reprinted with permission.

These three dimensions are important, and you want to keep them foremost in your mind as you develop your career-acceleration plan. In fact, we will go into a bit more detail about them later in the book.

That said, one problem with using these three dimensions alone is that they can paint a static picture. They do represent an ideal state, and it is certainly something we should work toward, but we need a guiding process to help us in the pursuit of that ideal state.

We drill down to the next level of granularity with the elements that go toward making up your potential career-acceleration plan. Just like an entrepreneur, you must take a comprehensive look at what is important in your life and what brings you the most joy and excitement. We refer to this segment as "Exploring Your Passion." The second section involves entering the marketplace with value, and we refer to it as "Discovering the Opportunities." Lastly, we realize that it is critical you are able to effectively communicate your skills and abilities in today's market, so this segment is titled "Telling Your Story." Each segment has separate processes that are aligned with what a business plan would contain if you were launching

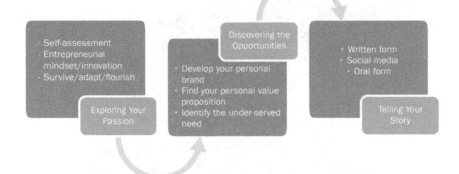

- Self-assessment
- Entrepreneurial mindset/innovation
- Survive/adapt/flourish

Exploring Your Passion

Discovering the Opportunities

- Develop your personal brand
- Find your personal value proposition
- Identify the under-served need

- Written form
- Social media
- Oral form

Telling Your Story

FIGURE 1.2. CAREER ACCELERATOR.

your business, but these processes are specifically tailored to be appropriate for someone who is launching a personal career-acceleration plan. The graphic in figure 1.2 depicts these three segments, which should be viewed collectively instead of on a hierarchical basis.

LEARN TO EXPLORE YOUR PASSIONS

The first segment is on exploring your passion and contains three different elements. You want to be able to give yourself time to reflect and develop a personal approach that will serve you. The items in this section will help you do the following:

Perform a critical **self-assessment** so that you are able to use assessment tools as well as proactively engage with others whom you trust and who will give you honest and candid feedback about your abilities. It is important for you to develop the ability and willingness to be open to hearing what others say about you and to be able to take that information and channel it toward your ideal career strategy.

Develop a deeper understanding of what it means to have an entrepreneurial mind-set and embrace the concept of **I Incorporated**.

Learn to develop short-term, intermediate, and long-term goals so you can **survive** in the short term, learn to **adapt** in the intermediate time frame, and ultimately **flourish** in your career pursuits.

LEARN TO DISCOVER THE OPPORTUNITIES

The next section focuses on discovering the opportunities in the market, and it too has three distinct elements. It is imperative that you are able to operate in a competitive marketplace, and these three elements will help you be more competitive in your endeavors. In these chapters, you will learn how to do the following:

Develop your **personal brand** so you consistently project what you want people to think about you and so others think of you within the desired context when they are thinking of people for a given position or opportunity.

Be able to be creative and develop your **personal value proposition** so you can adequately represent your value to the marketplace when you are given the opportunity to do so.

Be able to boldly look into the market and find the **under-served need**. If you are going to set yourself apart and be more valuable, you must be able to identify where you can have the biggest impact; hence, the under-served need.

Be able to creatively bring these three components together in a way that will create your unique **sweet spot** that will effectively differentiate you from the rest of the competition.

LEARN TO TELL YOUR STORY IN A COMPELLING MANNER

The final section relates to how you tell your personal story. You have done the work in creating a solid understanding of your personal abilities and desires and have also done a great job of understanding the potential opportunities and how you can bring value to those opportunities. Now you need to effectively tell others about your ability to contribute to these opportunities.

You will become much more effective in telling your personal story by doing the following:

Develop the key **written media** that you need to tell your story. Your resume and cover letter are key in this section, as are your business card and any other written material, which must all convey the same message. These written forms must discuss your value and how you can contribute to the appropriate market opportunity.

Take advantage of the opportunities provided through the use of **social media**. How we represent ourselves online is crucial in today's job scene. Learning how to effectively use the electronic tools that are available will go a long way in helping you communicate your personal brand in a thoughtful and compelling manner.

Learn how to tell a compelling story **orally** whenever you meet someone in person or on the phone. You need to develop a compelling elevator speech and be able to effectively connect with people in networking events. Also, it is absolutely crucial that you prepare your interview skills so that you are crystal clear about the nature of the under-served need and how your personal value proposition will serve that need.

Lastly, we will take you through a process that will provide you with a suitable framework in order to help you pull all these elements together into a personalized **career-acceleration plan**, which will serve you now and for the foreseeable future.

Part of the career-acceleration plan will allow you to apply the concepts of "rinse and repeat." Your career quest will never end. You will be pursuing these concepts for the rest of your professional life, but once you learn how to apply them, you will be able to rinse and repeat them again and again. Each time they will get stronger and will continuously help you in the pursuit of a viable, challenging, and engaging career.

CALL TO ACTION

Throughout the book and consistent with this overall approach will be a common theme encouraging you to take action and do things differently than you might have done them in the past. This is not about being passive and waiting for the results to come to you. It is about making the commitment to change your behavior and then following through on the required actions.

CHANGE YOUR BEHAVIOR

I want to take this opportunity to introduce you to a concept that many counselors use today in helping their clients change their behaviors. Essentially it is applying the concepts consistent with cognitive behavioral psychology and can be summarized in the following graphic.

Essentially the idea is that if you change your behavior, it will change how you think about something that will then change how you feel about it that will result in you wanting to change your behavior. The key is that it starts with a behavioral change, and as you go through the cycle, your thoughts and feelings will drive the new and desired behaviors.

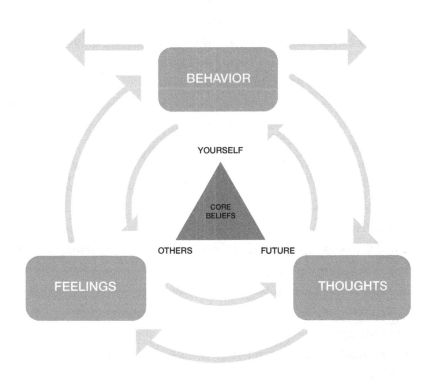

FIGURE 1.3. COGNITIVE BEHAVIORAL THERAPY
Copyright © Urstadt (CC BY-SA 3.0) at https://en.wikipedia.org/wiki/File:Depicting_basic_tenets_of_CBT.jpg.

Regarding your career quest, it will require that you start to behave differently. You will need to embrace the idea that you can market yourself effectively and you begin with new behaviors that can be reinforced by your thoughts and feelings.

It is these new behaviors that we will be discussing in this book. It will require you to understand them, practice them and then become more and more proficient in their execution.

BE RESOURCEFUL, RECEPTIVE AND READY

We all know that many college students around the country are having trouble launching viable careers upon graduation. In fact, some reports are saying that over 50% of recent college grads are going into jobs that they could have done with a high school diploma.

Now, there are lots of very dedicated professional people in the career field, trying to help students launch their careers, and the available resources are continuing to grow. Some examples are: different software applications to help connect students with employers, better use of video interviewing techniques and more networking and mock interview opportunities.

However, I have come to realize that the student has to be able to truly take advantage of these support structures in order to be successful. In short, they have to be resourceful, receptive and ready to take action.

If you find yourself in this situation, take a moment and think about how **resourceful** you truly are. Are you able to find networking events or mock interview opportunities? If not, put a plan in place to expand your degree of resourcefulness.

But simply being resourceful is not enough, you have to be **receptive** to the concepts that you are exploring. Are you viewing them from the traditional mind-set of making a resume and posting it to job boards, or do you truly have a different mind-set and are fully receptive to these new ways of pursuing a career?

And then, after you have considered your sense of resourcefulness and have committed to being receptive to the ideas, you have to take action. You have to be **ready** to make a change and pursue your prospects from a totally different paradigm. In essence, your degree of readiness will make all the difference in your career quest.

The bottom line is: strive to be <u>resourceful</u> and seek out new options. Strive to be <u>receptive</u> to the new ideas and do not judge them from an old paradigm and lastly, strive to be <u>ready</u> to take action and to make the commitment necessary to achieve success.

Do not accept that you will be a statistic and part of the 50% who are not able to capitalize on their college education. There is clearly an alternative. Be resourceful, be receptive and then be ready to take action.

CAREER PLAN DEVELOPMENT PROCESS

One thing that is important for you to realize is that this is a process, not an event. It is not about just doing one or two things and then launching a successful career. Now, it do not need to be a grueling process or one that is filled with uncertainty, but it does require you to think about what you want to change, identify the specific steps to take and then follow through on their attainment.

MAKE A COMMITMENT

Give yourself the benefit of making a commitment to do things differently. Give it some serious thought, but when you are ready, commit to yourself that you will, indeed, change your behavior.

WRITE IT DOWN

In the "Additional Resources" section of this chapter, I will list several resources for you to use in the development of your career plan. One is my web page that has a career plan template on it for you to use. Regardless of what tool you use, take some time to document your plan in a way that makes sense to you and can be used to track your progress.

JUST DO IT

We have all heard that expression from Nike and it rings very true in this setting. You have to plan but more importantly, you have to execute the plan. Think about it, make the commitment, and then take action.

VIEW THE RESULTS

Periodically, set aside some time to see how you are progressing against the plan. If you build the plan but never review the progress, you will miss the opportunity to review, improve and continue to grow.

RINSE AND REPEAT

We will talk a little more about this later in the book, but the idea is that this is an ongoing process, and you will want to do it over and over again. Each time you do it, it will get stronger and more productive for you. Know that it is a process that you will be pursuing throughout your professional career.

ADDITIONAL RESOURCES

One key resource that I want to introduce you to in this chapter is my personal website: https://sites.google.com/a/umich.edu/mike-callahan/college-students Take a look at it and see if it can help you. We do run periodic online sessions covering the I Inc. content and advertise these opportunities on the website. There is not charge other than to have a copy of this book.

Also, feel free to connect to my LinkedIn account. I frequently posted current announcements and updates on this site: https://www.linkedin.com/in/mikecallahancareerhelp

We will also include other additional resources for each chapter that will give you access to more information beyond what is covered in that respective chapter.

NOW WHAT?

Let's briefly review the chapter. We talked about the changing workplace, the free market economics, a guiding context for you to use, a call to action, an overview of career-acceleration plan, a process to follow and finally, some additional resources that you might want to check out.

Here are some suggestions about ways for you to further your understanding of these concepts:

1. Take a look at the following website and identify three or four ways that these changes will impact you directly.
http://www.forbes.com/sites/jacobmorgan/2014/08/22/the-future-of-work-how-millennials-are-changing-the-workplace/
2. Make a list of three pros and three cons of the free market system and discuss them with someone in your personal network.
3. Critically review the triangle and identify one or two ways that each of the three sides can help inform career-related decisions that you might be making.
4. Go back and review the nine elements of the career-acceleration plan and see if you can come up with one tangible way for you to strengthen your abilities within that specific element.

Throughout the book, we will explore ways for you to apply the concepts in your own career quest. It is not about memorizing a list of details and then repeating them on a test. Instead, it is about taking these concepts, internalizing them so that they serve you, and then applying them directly within your own career strategies. The more you can learn to use them in that manner, the more they will serve you now and for the rest of your professional career.

REFERENCES

Bolles, Richard N. *What Color Is Your Parachute? A Practical Manual for Job-Hunters and Career-Changers*. New York: Random House, 2013.

Friedman, Thomas L. *The World Is Flat: A Brief History of the Twenty-First Century*. New York: Farrar, Straus and Giroux, 2005.

Morgan, Jacob. "The Future of Work: How Millennials Are Changing the Workplace." *Forbes*, August 22, 2014. http://www.forbes.com/sites/jacobm-organ/2014/08/22/the-future-of-work-how-millennials-are-changing-the-workplace.

Pew Research Center. *College Days Reconsidered* February 14, 2014

Thoreau, Henry David. *Civil Disobedience and Other Essays*. Mineola, NY: Dover Thrift Editions, 1993.

SECTION 2.

EXPLORING your PASSION

INTRODUCTION

The next three chapters delve into the core of what makes you tick. In order to be successful in today's economy, someone with an entrepreneurial mind-set needs to be clear about who they are, what their personal styles are, what their interest are, and how can they best ensure that what they do is in line with their personality.

Chapter 2 is all about self-assessment. As an individual who is pursuing your own career aspirations, it is critical that you have a solid understanding of your personality, preferences, strengths, and weaknesses in order to know how to pursue opportunities that are most in line with your interests. We will explore several different tools as well as give you a framework in which to operate to help you deepen your personal understanding of yourself.

Chapter 3 expands on the whole idea of thinking like an entrepreneur. Again, it is not about starting your own company but more about embracing the idea that you are in charge of your career. There is a concept called self-efficacy, whereby people who are strong in this construct are confident that regardless of what they confront, they will persevere. That is the fundamental idea of Chapter 3. Learn to think in such a way so that when they world gives you a lemon, you make lemonade.

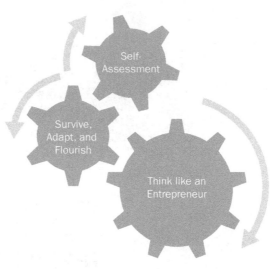

FIGURE 2.0. MAKING YOUR PASSION WORK FOR YOU.

Chapter 4 delves into the idea of surviving, adapting, and flourishing. Throughout life, you will find yourself in situations that require you to survive while you look for ways to adapt and ultimately flourish. We will help you develop a deeper understanding of that concept, along with some tools that can help you throughout the journey.

The next section will shift the focus to be more externally driven, but for now, let's zero in on how you think, the types of preferences you have in order to maximize your potential for success and ultimately, how you tackle adversity.

2 Self-Assessment

KNOW YOURSELF

The first step in our entrepreneurial context development helps you understand how you fit into the overall scheme. What are the priorities that pull you in different directions? What do you love to do? What do you find yourself doing when you lose track of time? In essence, what do you bring to the market that is valuable, consistent with your personal goals and aspirations, and something you literally want to get up each morning and do, potentially for a very long time?

The concepts we discuss in this book are important to high school students trying to decide which field of study they want to pursue, to people in midcareer looking for more meaningful opportunities, all the way to individuals who have "retired" from a former career and are now looking for something to pursue in the final chapter of their professional lives. It is important to take the time to truly know yourself, and to learn to deal with the challenges that we are constantly bombarded by and the external stimuli that cause us to take different approaches.

We may have family members who encourage us to take a certain approach, or peers or even the entertainment industry will help drive our decisions. It has been argued that different TV shows can influence the number of students who decide to pursue a specific career, based on the popularity of the show.

We all want guidance. We want to be fulfilled and enjoy our work, but part of the problem comes from the fact that we do not have sufficient information to make an informed decision. In the absence of that information, we are swayed by external influencers who are trying to help but can often push us in a direction that might not be best for us. The following sections will give you a context and some specific steps that you can take to help you with this challenge.

IDENTIFY YOUR CAREER OBJECTIVES

Take a little time and think about what your career objectives truly are related to your college pursuits. Are you after the grade, an education, experience, a degree or what? I have been teaching at a university for over 10 years and there is one phenomenon that continues to baffle me.

If you bought a cup of coffee, and the barista only filled the cup half-full, you would be very unhappy. If you went to a movie and the theater manager announced half way through the movie that he was going to let you leave and not spend the next 60 minutes watching the end of the movie, you would go ballistic.

And yet, it seems that for many of my classes, if I did that with my students, I have this feeling that they would gladly accept it. I could give them half a cup of the lesson plan, or only run the class for half of the scheduled time, and I think that many of them would be satisfied, and probably give me smiley faces on "Rate my Professor."

What is it with that? Am I wrong? Would there be an uprising, or have we created a system whereby the outcome of a grade is all that really matters?

I know that this is an example in the extreme, but I still feel that that sentiment exists to a fairly large extent.

Now, I do not think this is the students' fault. The blame lies with those who have created, and continue to reinforce the system, and I am one of them. We just need to change it, but that task is extremely daunting, and I am somewhat perplexed at where to begin.

I mention this simply to challenge your way of thinking if you are looking at a college education in terms of earning a grade and ultimately getting the diploma, with the belief, that the diploma will magically open career opportunities to you.

It is imperative that you do not allow yourself to be following the minimalist grade plan but rather demand from yourself, and your professors, the highest level of developmental experience that you can handle. Learning how to relate to people, to understand their needs and wants and then gaining a better understanding of how you can market your abilities will truly set you apart from the competition.

Another way to approach this idea is covered in the question our parents and relatives have consistently asked us over the years. What do you want to do when you grow up? I am sure most everyone heard that question over and over as a child. Unfortunately, our responses at the time were limited to what our parents or family members did or maybe what we saw on TV. Or maybe there were some ideas that we felt were heroic callings, like being a jet pilot or a fireman. There is nothing wrong with those aspirations. They are certainly worth considering, but the world is way too big to be limited to just what we have observed when we try to answer this question.

How do we go about figuring this out in a thoughtful, reflective manner when we are only exposed to a small set of potential opportunities? It might be a good idea to let that entrepreneurial mind-set kick in again. Instead of choosing from a finite list of potential opportunities of which we are currently aware, maybe we should start with a much broader approach in terms of the general values we want to explore.

The key is not to allow your thinking to be limited by prior experiences. Treat the situation as one of abundance, not of scarcity. When we see the world from a place of scarcity, we immediately begin to zero in on those things we know we can accomplish. However, when we approach it from a place of abundance, anything is possible!

Read on. We will continue to develop these concepts as you learn more about yourself through further self-assessment processes.

CAREER DILEMMA

To begin your journey, take a little time and get explicit about anything that is causing conflict in your career aspirations. We use the term *career dilemma* to help nail those conflicts down.

A career dilemma is something that we possess throughout our working lives and into retirement. It basically describes the dilemma we face when we are pulled in different directions. Diane Ducat, in her book *Turning Points*, notes: "A career dilemma arises from a tangled set of interrelated career and education issues that you face." Your career dilemma is made up of the doubts and questions you have about the direction of your career or education; we all have career dilemmas through our lives.

It is pretty simple to understand the idea of a career dilemma, but it can be quite confusing when you try to work through the different trade-offs for yourself. Some other drivers of your personal career dilemma might be:

- Fearing that your job is going away but not being sure what to do about it,
- Feeling dissatisfied with your current job but feeling trapped,
- Pursuing a career that your family wants for you but you know is not what you want,
- Being in a job that does not capitalize on your true abilities,
- Being inexperienced in your new role,
- Being in a role that frequently fluctuates from high pressure to low motivation, or
- Feeling trapped but not being able to take action.

Any of these sound familiar? Like I said earlier, we are constantly affected by our career dilemmas. It is hard to imagine a day going by that at least one of these items doesn't float across your consciousness. They are constantly there, pulling us in different directions and challenging us to respond accordingly.

WAYS TO RESOLVE YOUR
CAREER DILEMMAS

The key to resolve these dilemmas has to do with how we choose to handle these pressures and how we can make the changes that will help us further along the path of our career aspirations.

The basic question to answer is: How do I choose to resolve my career dilemmas in a way that will serve me, bring value into my life, ensure I have a secure future, and provide me with a constant source of challenge and inspiration? Again, it may sound a bit overwhelming, but if you go back, take a page from the previous chapter, and approach this with an entrepreneurial mind-set, the answer may be easier than you think.

First, take it one step at a time. Your career dilemmas will continue to evolve, but you can only work on the current one at this time. Take a moment to write it down and begin to identify the advantages and disadvantages of choosing different options. As you work through this chapter, you will have many opportunities to explore different strategies that can help you with that dilemma.

It may be a dilemma over which major to pursue in college or whether you should move to a new location. Or it may be a dilemma over taking a new position that would offer less compensation but potentially better experience. It may even be that you know you do not like what you are currently doing, but you do not know how to proceed to the next step in your professional career.

Once you take the time to write it down, along with the pros and cons of different choices, take a moment and allow yourself to enter into the entrepreneurial mind-set. Ask yourself how an entrepreneur would decide which option to take. Would he or she seek out more information from customer surveys (informational interviews, research via the internet, and so on)? How about taking "baby steps" and trying one of the options on a limited basis in a test market? Or maybe trying to get into the mind-set of a potential buyer and seeing how it would feel to purchase this product?

The key is that once you enter the entrepreneurial mind-set, you can be much more objective about the decision, and it begins to open up potential options that you might not have otherwise considered. When you think about it from your personal mind-set, you are caught up in the emotion and trying to make a decision that is best for your psyche. However, when you are in the entrepreneurial mind-set, your focus shifts to one of maximizing the value of the decision. You can be much more objective when you look at the dilemma from this perspective.

For instance, if the dilemma were to consider taking a new position at less money but more opportunity, the personal mind-set may focus more on the financial loss and possibly a loss in personal prestige, whereas the entrepreneurial mind-set will be able to see it as an investment for the future and might be more open to the option of going with a new opportunity.

The key is the mind-set with which you approach the dilemma. You must still do your research, evaluate different options, get input from family and friends and carefully weigh the different outcomes. However, if you think like an entrepreneur, you will make decisions that help you move your career-acceleration plan along a path that is much more akin to creating a business plan than simply getting stuck and trying to wade through different emotionally laden options.

Remember, you are dealing with a logical and fair but infinitely objective free market. In order to function most effectively in this market, you too must be objective. An entrepreneurial mind-set will give you the greatest chance at achieving that level of objectivity in your decisions.

We have further identified eight different ways to help you be better able to cope with your personal dilemma. However, they are all based on a couple of key concepts. The first is that you feel open to exploring new options. If you are convinced that you know what you want to do for the rest of your life, then this approach might not work well for you. The second prerequisite is that you are open to the idea of abundance and not scarcity. If you believe that you have unlimited potential, then you do. If you believe that you are constrained, then you are. Whatever you believe in will become true in your life, so strive to believe in an abundance mind-set. The third constraint is that you are willing to let go of your current assumptions and work on exploring new assumptions. You will never discover a new place if you are afraid to lose sight of the current shore. It takes risk and courage, but the rewards will be worth the effort. Assuming that you are able to accept these prerequisites, let's explore the different options available to you.

MEDITATION

We are often so caught up in our daily activities that we do not take time to get into a quiet moment and let our mind explore possibilities. This is not a book on effective meditation, but I do know enough about the concept to be able to use it effectively from time to time. The idea is to simply commit to a period of time on a regular basis in which you give yourself permission to let go of the daily pressures and allow yourself to be at peace. It is amazing how much can become clear to you if you just take the time to let it become manifest in your life. Get into a secluded physical place, give yourself permission to relax, take some steps to quiet your mind, and allow yourself the pure relaxation that comes with meditation.

When you are in this state, pay attention to what your mind is telling you. Listen for clues about how certain things make you feel. Essentially, listen to your inner voice. We tend to crowd it out with all the activities in our lives, so take some time to let it be heard. And listen to what it is saying.

MINDFULNESS

It is so easy to get caught up in the daily activities that occupy our time and our thoughts. We spend so much time thinking about the next class, or the person I just met, or what I am going to be doing tonight that we often lose sight of what is truly important in our lives

Being mindful is nothing more than being completely present in the moment. Take a time out. Listen to your feelings and thoughts and allow them to guide you instead of trying to do something based on your perception of what someone else may want for you. Give yourself permission to truly be quiet, to listen and then be guided by what your mind is telling you.

PERSONAL REFLECTION

The following is a brief exercise that will help you begin to explore possible values that are important to you. Go through the following list and circle the ten items that are most important to you in your life. Then, after you have done that, eliminate five of those ten. Lastly, get it down to three.

Accountability	Fame	Personal development
Action	Family	Personal liberties
Activity	Fast paced Freedom	Physical challenge
Artistic	Friendships	Power
Authenticity	Fortune	Privacy
Authority	Happiness	Public service
Challenge	Help people	Quality
Change	Honesty	Recognition
Collaboration	Independence	Relationships
Community	Influence	Religion
Competence	Integrity	Reputation
Competition	Intelligence	Respect
Constructive criticism	Involvement	Responsibility
Country	Job satisfaction	Security
Creativity	Knowledge	Self-respect
Decisiveness	Leadership	Service
Democracy	Location	Stability
Ecology	Love	Status
Effectiveness	Loyalty	Structure
Efficiency	Merit	Teamwork
Ethics	Money	Truth
Excellence	Nature	Wealth
Excitement	Order	Wisdom
Expertise	Peace	

These three items represent your current personal starting point. They will evolve over time, so you might want to repeat the process from time to time. However, they do represent what is important to you at this time and, as such, should be given due consideration in your ongoing development of a career strategy.

We will refer to these as the three key values in subsequent activities. By the way, do not worry if you are not sure if these really are the top three values you want to pursue at this time. They simply represent a starting point. As you work with them, either it will become clear that they represent what you want out of life, or doubt will creep in and you will want to change. Either of these outcomes is acceptable. You should treat these key values as a work in progress and either continue to refine them or tweak the list and identify other items. The key is to get started and also to allow yourself to think beyond what you have currently experienced.

Actually, a lot of people struggle with this concept. They say this is all well and good, but they need a job and cannot just pursue their dreams. It is unfortunate if you look at it from that perspective, because you can pursue your dreams, and you deserve to do so! Your dreams may be realized in a way you have not yet even begun to comprehend, but don't quit before you have given them a chance. Your career aspirations will manifest themselves with you in ways you cannot even imagine at this time. Allow yourself the opportunity to dream, to embrace values worthy of your efforts and begin the journey to a much more fulfilled and challenging life.

Another way to approach this concept is to simply take out a blank sheet of paper and write down everything that you would associated with a possible career outcome. It might be things like: travel a lot, or work close to home, or make a lot of money, or even be a manager, or the alternative is to be an individual performer. The key is that you want to make the list as exhaustive as possible and think about all of the different options that could be associated with a potential career. Do not try to edit any of them at this time. Just use free association and come up with a comprehensive list.

Once you have the list completed, then go back through it and identify those elements that are most important. Place a 1 by those. Place a 2 by those that have some importance and then a 3 by those that are irrelevant in your career aspirations.

After you have done that, then go back, review the #1 priorities and think about what you have been doing regarding your career. See if you have been doing things that are consistently with those priorities or possibly doing somethings that might be in conflict with them.

Use it as a tool to review what you are currently doing but also, you can review it frequently to see if you are on track or if things are evolving the way you desire.

I used this approach several years ago and built my list, thought about it for a while and then filed it away and thought that I had forgotten about it. I pulled it out several years later, and everything that I had identified as a #1 priority was in my current role, and all of the 2s and 3s were not. The process works for me, and I would hope it would work for you. Take some time, think about all of the possible options available to you, prioritize them and then let them flow into your life.

Regardless of which technique you use, either off of the long list provided or you building your own list, I believe it can go a long way in helping you achieve what is truly important in your life.

TAKE SOME ASSESSMENTS

There are many different types of personality assessments that might be of benefit to you. Some of the most common ones are listed below:

Myers-Briggs

Myers-Briggs focuses on helping you better understand your personality preferences. It will help you understand how you choose to gain energy. It will give you insight into how you prefer to gather information as well as how you prefer to make decisions. It will also give you some further insight into how you prefer to relate to the outside world. Taking this assessment helps you better understand your preferences but also can give you some further insight into how other people prefer to achieve these outcomes. There is no right or wrong approach. It can be very helpful if you are working in a team with others have taken the assessment. We are all different, and this assessment acknowledges the differences but also gives you some valuable guidance in terms of how to use it to guide your decisions going forward.

Other Assessment Tools

Strong Interest Inventory uses John Holland's taxonomy of Realistic, Investigative, Artistic, Social, Enterprising, and Conventional psychological interests. Using this inventory can help someone understand the type of environment, and ultimately the type of career, to which they might be best suited.

FOCUS 2, which may be available through your college's career center, combines self-assessment, career and major exploration, decision making, and action planning in one tool.

Strengths Finder, a tool developed by Marcus Buckingham and Donald O. Clifton, is explained in their book called *Now, Discover Your Strengths* and helps you identify your specific strengths and how you might be able to better capitalize on them.

All these tools, and many others, can provide you with additional insight into your personality, your interests, and your skills. (You can find more resources in the "Additional Resources" section of this chapter.)

They will also provide you with suggestions or ideas about the kinds of careers in which people with a similar propensity have been successful. It is a good idea to use one or two of these tools, but do not become so obsessed that you try to use all of them in the hope of having complete clarity about what you should be doing with your life.

These assessments are well developed and have significant research to back them, so do use them. But keep in mind that they cannot tell you what to do. Use them to better complete your self-assessment; but also tap into the other suggestions that we offer to help you develop a comprehensive sense of who you are and what makes you special.

DO SOME NETWORKING

We will go into much more detail in both chapters 7 and 11 regarding networking and ways to do it more effectively, but for now just give some thought to talking with people to better understand what they do. The broader your reference base is, the easier it is to think about different roles that you could perform. We said earlier that we are often limited by our friends, our parents, or maybe even watching a few shows on TV to get ideas about potential careers. Networking is a way to exponentially expand that reference base.

Seek out opportunities to network with either local chambers of commerce or professional organizations that might be of interest to you personally. Go to the events and feel free both to introduce yourself and to ask the other attendees what they do for a living. People go to networking events to network, and people like to talk about themselves. If you choose to take advantage of these opportunities, you will significantly expand your potential options to consider.

SEEK OUT SOME INFORMATIONAL INTERVIEWS

Another option that we will explore more fully in chapter 7 is called an informational interview, which is an effective way to learn about different options by asking people in your area of interest about what they do for a living. However, using this type of interview is not the same as looking for a job. Its sole purpose is to give you a chance to gain some information about a potential career, industry, location, or anything else you want to explore. Feel free to reach out to different people in jobs that might be of interest to you and ask them for an informational interview.

Be clear that you are not asking for a job but simply the opportunity to inquire about what it takes to be successful in their career, industry, or location. Again, people like to talk about themselves and what they do, and this too can provide you with some invaluable information about potential career paths.

This is not an attempt to get into a meeting with someone and then spring your resume on them. That is not what you asked for when you requested an informational interview, and it is not what they are expecting. It actually violates the integrity of your request. You can certainly bring a copy of your resume to the interview, and if they ask you for it, that is wonderful. But you cannot use the interview as an opportunity to ask for a job.

In an informational interview, you are asking for help. You are asking the individual to help you understand what is valued in the industry. If the individual is involved in hiring decisions, he or she can be a great source of information about what companies are looking for in terms of skills and abilities, as well as what kinds of experiences are important.

There are many ways that you can secure an informational interview. If you are on LinkedIn, you can identify contacts through it. You might find someone who is a second-level contact, but you could still reach out to him or her, mention that you are both associates of the first-level contact, and ask for an informational interview.

If you want to dive deeper into the whole process, there is a great book called *The 2-Hour Job Search* by Steve Dalton. This book will give you a ton of processes and procedures to pursue informational interviews and expand your network. This book is good for an individual who knows what he or she wants to do and is looking for specific contacts. If you are not there yet, do not worry. This book might not be what you want right now, but when you are ready, it is a great resource.

In the meantime, find people in decision-making roles in firms who do the kind of work you think you would like to do and seek out informational interviews with these people. Keep track of your contacts, send them a thank-you message after they meet with you, and keep them in your personal network going forward.

RESEARCH OCCUPATIONAL OUTLOOK

You can make the quest much more effective if you are open to exploring options that allow you to see how you can bring value to the marketplace. Remember, the key is that you want to do things that are consistent with your personal values, but you also want to do things that are valuable to the external world. Therefore, as you review the different databases, always keep in mind how a specific role is able to deliver, or not deliver, value to its respective clients. The more you do that, the easier it will be for you to discuss that value when you are engaged in subsequent conversations with recruiters.

Let's get into some of the sources of data. I recommend a great starting point: the *Occupational Outlook Handbook* (http://www.bls.gov/OCO.) It is published by the US government and has a wealth of information you can use to explore different careers, skill sets, training programs, education requirements, compensation expectations, and projected job growth in various fields. Also, as you peruse the information, be sure to look at the O*NET database referenced on this website; you can also explore the database online via a search engine such as Google.

Between these two sources and the subsequent searches, you will be able to find almost anything you need to match your current skill sets with potential job opportunities. Also, you may find you are missing the kinds of experience that would qualify you for a certain role. That is great information! If the role is something consistent with your values and you possess some of the skills but not all of them, this is a great starting point for the further development of your career-acceleration plan.

VOLUNTEER TO GET YOUR HANDS DIRTY

The eighth option is to look for ways to actually experience some of the work that you might wind up doing. You might job shadow someone for a day or two to observe what they do. Another possibility is to actually volunteer to get into the environment and perform some of the work, or some element of it, for which you are currently qualified to perform. The idea is that we can read or hear about different options, but getting into the middle of it and actually experiencing some of the real work will help you decide how interested you are in that arena.

Try not to dismiss this option without giving it some serious consideration. You can learn a lot about doing some of the work that you are considering for your career. It is one thing to think about something and talk with others about doing it, but it is an entirely different thing when you actually do it. And the beauty of volunteering is that it is easy for you to get experience, especially if you reach out to professional organizations or other groups who rely on volunteers to pursue their mission. You will get the chance to try it before you buy it and even build some solid relationships with others in your area of interest.

ADDITIONAL RESOURCES

If any of the above suggestions resonate with you, I would hope that you would consider dong some further research on the internet. To help get that started, here are some resources for self-assessment tools:

http://www.halogensoftware.com/blog/self-appraisal-examples-to-use-as-guidance-or-inspiration

http://www.capterra.com/sem-compare/performance-appraisal-software?headline=Top%2010%20Self%20Appraisal%20Software&gclid=CJOC2cbgnNECFRCQaQodHAYICQ

And here are some regarding informational interviews:

https://www.livecareer.com/quintessential/informational-interview-questions

http://bestcareermatch.com/interview-questions

And lastly, some potential volunteer opportunities that can help you get your hands dirty.

http://www.volunteermatch.org/

https://www.volunteer.gov/

Self-assessment is clearly a contact sport. It requires you to take the initiative but also follow through on the assessments. Simply saying that you think you understand yourself may not be enough. Take advantage of these opportunities and do a deeper dive into understanding who you really are, what is important to you, what are your personal values and what will you aspire to become regardless of the obstacles that face you along the way. As you explore these suggestions, you can rely on a myriad of tools on the internet to help you prepare for a meeting or do further research after you have connected with someone. However, before you begin the quest, revisit the idea of an entrepreneurial mind-set and remind yourself of what that means to you.

One of the tools we will discuss more in chapter 10 is an electronic portfolio, along with other ways to tell your story using social media. The reason I mention it now is to reinforce one more idea. As you pursue any of these suggestions, be sure to keep good notes of what you discover. That information will help inform you regarding future career decisions, and it will provide a great basis for you to use when you are developing your personal story for potential recruiters. Remember, you are always in the selling mode, so even if you are researching and reflecting about what is important to you, it is highly possible that you will also be communicating some of those elements to future employers.

Explore the online information. It is vast and continues to expand on a daily basis. Keep in mind that you want to explore options you have had some experience with and that are consistent with your values, build on your current skills and abilities, and offer you a chance to build your track record within that specific domain.

NOW WHAT?

The idea in this chapter is to take the time to understand not only your passions but also where you do not shine. Therefore, there are two types of action steps to consider: identifying your passions and identifying areas where you may not flourish. Let's start with the former and work to the latter.

It is important to do a survey of where you currently stand, so take some time to answer the following questions:

1. Do I truly love my current job?
2. If I am in college, do I believe that my current major will lead me to what I want to be doing?
3. Do my activities outside of work and school contribute to my personal happiness and self-satisfaction?

If you are not sure about your answer to any of these questions, then you have a great place to start. Keep them in mind as you pursue some of the following suggestions.

1. Commit to a regular process of meditation or some other way to give you the chance to let your mind become quiet and to prepare you to be open to possible alternatives.
2. Do some personal reflection. Use the list of traits mentioned earlier in the chapter to identify the top three or four values that are important to you. Commit to an ongoing process of reviewing the list every six to twelve months.
3. Take some assessments. Look for opportunities to take a few of the assessments that serve you, and give some focused thought to what they are telling you.

4. Attend some networking events. Figure out a schedule that works for you and become a regular attendee at events that will help you learn more about possible options for your career.
5. Commit to a regular process of participating in informational interviews. Pay attention to what you are learning and keep good records.
6. Get your hands dirty. Look for opportunities to experiment and do some of the work that you might have an interest in pursuing. Even things like student organizations or other volunteer operations will give you the chance to try some things out and see if they fit your interests.
7. Learn to use the internet and research the pages we discussed in the book as well as your own topics. The wealth of information that is available to you for the asking will provide you with significant insight into potential options to consider.
8. Ask a close friend to give you feedback on how he or she perceives you and your key strengths and interests. This can be difficult, but a true friend can give you an honest perspective that is priceless. If you have this option, I strongly recommend that you take advantage of it.
9. Take some time to write down what you love, what you want your life to be about, and what your vision for a full and happy life is.

It is important for an entrepreneur to periodically review what his or her company is all about, and it is equally important for you to do the same. Take some time, write it down, give yourself the chance to reflect and adjust based on what you learn, and make the commitment to continue to do this on an ongoing basis.

REFERENCES

Buckingham, Marcus, and Donald O. Clifton. *Now, Discover Your Strengths*. New York: Simon & Schuster, 2001.

Dalton, Steve. *The 2-Hour Job Search: Using Technology to Get the Right Job, Faster*. New York: Random House, 2012.

Ducat, Diane. *Turning Points: Your Career Decision-Making Guide*. Boston, MA: Pearson Education, 2012.

US Department of Labor, Bureau of Labor Statistics. *Occupational Outlook Handbook*. http://www.bls.gov/ooh.

Talent Space Blog by Halogen Software, *Self-Appraisal Examples to Use as Guidance or Inspiration*, http://www.halogensoftware.com/blog/self-appraisal-examples-to-use-as-guidance-or-inspiration

Capterra, *10 Self-Appraisal Software Tools* http://www.capterra.com/sem-compare/performance-appraisal-software?headline=Top%2010%20Self%20Appraisal%20Software&gclid=CJOC2cbgnNECFRCQaQodHAYICQ

Quintessential, *Informational Interviewing: 200 Informational Interview Sample Questions* https://www.livecareer.com/quintessential/informational-interview-questions

Best-Career-Match.com 20 Interview Questions to Ask in Informational Interviews http://bestcareermatch.com/interview-questions

Volunteermatch.org We *bring good people and good causes together* http://www.volunteermatch.org/

Volunteer.gov *America's Natural and Cultural Resources Volunteer Portal* https://www.volunteer.gov/

3
Developing an Entrepreneurial aka More Empowered Mind-Set

KEY CONCEPT

YOU ARE YOUR OWN BUSINESS OF ONE!

The concept we use throughout the book is really quite simple. Essentially, it calls on you to approach your career-planning process with an entrepreneurial mind-set. I have chosen to call this concept "I Incorporated." Actually, Tom Peters wrote about it several years ago in his book *Thriving on Chaos*, and there have been many authors recently who have discussed how individuals must take control of their careers and even potentially participate in a "free agent nation," in the words of Daniel H. Pink. More recently, Reid Hoffman, cofounder and chair of LinkedIn, and Ben Casnocha wrote a book called *The Start-Up of You*, in which they describe some of the best practices of start-up ventures in Silicon Valley and how you might be able to apply those concepts to your own career.

The point is that the idea of being your own business has been around for a few years but has often been applied in environments where being a traditional entrepreneur was more expected and supported. Although we obviously continue to support and encourage those concepts, we want to take this idea and make it applicable to everyone who is in today's job market. Whether you work for a large company or a small one, or for the government or even in the nonprofit sector, you are in business for yourself. You are your own business of one, and we encourage you to embrace that concept and make it part of your fundamental belief structure.

You may be reading all sorts of suggestions about creating your personal brand, learning how to make an elevator speech, or building your personal portfolio. These are all part of the story, but the key concept for you to understand is: In order to be empowered in your personal career development, you must choose to be entrepreneurial and use the I Incorporated concept to provide a context for all of these principles.

Successful businesses all need some form of a business plan. A plan might be thoroughly documented, or it might reside significantly inside of the founder's head, but all plans have some form of vision and strategy to pursue that vision. We take that concept and build on it to support your career quest. Essentially, we believe that building and executing a business plan is similar to the concepts and challenges associated with building a career-acceleration plan.

What is unique about this approach is we use the processes entrepreneurs use to build a business plan and transfer them into the context of creating a career-acceleration plan. To build a business, you must identify an under-served need, develop a plan to serve that need, develop a strategy to market your product or service, and lastly, ensure your customer is satisfied. To build a career-acceleration plan, you must identify where there is an opportunity, develop a plan to be able to respond to that opportunity, develop a plan to market yourself, and lastly, ensure you are providing value to the market.

To embrace this concept, you must make a fundamental change in your attitude toward your job-search strategy. This can be uncomfortable and is definitely outside the traditional mind-set of creating a resume and hoping someone will give you a job. Entrepreneurs have a clear understanding of the value their product or service has in the marketplace, and you too must have a clear understanding of your value to the marketplace.

However, before you panic and say you are not ready to go out and start your own business, take a breath and think about what people do when they start their own business and then think about how you might transfer those behaviors into your own career pursuits. Also, realize that even though you may not want to actually start your own business, in reality you are in business for yourself. This is the fundamental difference that exists in the market today. In the past you could go to work for a company and remain there for your entire career. That has totally changed. You should expect to move into many different roles throughout your career, possibly in one or many different companies, many of which have not yet even been developed.

Allow yourself to approach the market as an entrepreneur. Again, treat potential employers as potential clients. Regardless of where you choose to work, this context will serve you in your initial job search as well as throughout your professional life. Once you begin to approach your career-planning process using the same concepts you would use to develop a business plan, you will be able to draw from the experiences of entrepreneurs and apply those lessons to your own career strategy.

As we further develop the entire package of somewhat nontraditional career-planning tools and techniques within the I Incorporated context, you will be able to constantly ask yourself a few simple questions. If I were starting/running a business, how would I handle this specific challenge/opportunity? How would I articulate the value I bring through this skill or ability? Why would someone want to pay for this service? How do I communicate the value in a compelling and interesting manner? Successful business owners deal with these issues all the time. In order for you to be successful, they must become part of your personal repertoire and constantly serve as inspiration and insight into your career decisions.

BUSINESS PLAN/CAREER PLAN

There is another quotation by Steven Jobs that I feel is very relevant to consider at this time. Essentially, he is credited with saying: " "Your work is going to fill a large part of your life, and the only way to be truly satisfied is to do what you believe is great work. And the only way to do great work is to love what you do. If you haven't found it yet, keep looking. Don't settle. As with all matters of the heart, you'll know when you find it." Take that idea, embrace it and then develop a plan to make it a reality.

As I mentioned earlier, we use the concepts in a traditional business plan to help inform the kinds of things you need to do to develop a viable career plan but it goes further than that. In order for your plan to be successful, I want you to take a moment and reflect on the following list of characteristics that are generally associated with a successful entrepreneur. Now, it would be unrealistic to expect that any of us are strong in all of these areas. We are going to be very well developed in some, and others will need further attention. That is OK. We are all human, and to expect perfection is unrealistic. However, it is good to have an idea of what we are striving to become as we work through the concepts of building our own career plan.

When we review some of the literature about what it takes to be a successful entrepreneur or someone who is successful at being an entrepreneur of their career, we find the following items to be very important. People in this arena:

- Set personal goals
- Are strongly committed to the outcomes
- Possess a spirit of adventure
- Have a strong drive to achieve results
- Are self-confident
- Are a self-starter
- Are innovative, creative and persistent
- Do not give up easily
- Are a positive thinker
- Push themselves to improve
- Embrace uncertainty
- Take smart risks
- Are not afraid to get their hands dirty
- Love what they do

It is a very tough list to aspire to become, and yet once you do, you will never have to hope that someone will give you a job. Instead you will have the drive, passion and commitment to find your way and identify the kinds of opportunities that truly will feed your soul and be consistent with what you are truly capable of becoming.

Review the list. Identify those that you are strong in and those that need improvement. Continue to build the ones that are strong and develop a strategy to accommodate those that are not that strong.

PLAYING THE "BLAME GAME"

One thing you must accept right from the beginning is that you are responsible for your career. It is not the responsibility of your spouse, partner, boss, coworker, politician, teacher, or anyone else in your life. It is totally up to you, period! If something happens in your career and you find yourself in a difficult position, it is up to you to deal with it. No one else is responsible!

Too many people hit a bump in their career and want to play the blame game. They blame the politicians in Washington who are cutting back on programs, or those workers in (pick a country) who are willing to do what they do for less money, or the people they work with who are holding them back. If you are going to benefit from this book, you cannot play the blame game. Suck it up. Take responsibility for your career and make it happen.

I fully realize that if I were reading this book several years ago, I might have stopped right here. After all, it was my current company's leadership that was to blame when I lost my job, not me. I was busy doing what I had always done, and the company changed the game on me. I had built a successful career as a midlevel executive within the company and did not understand how or what had happened.

In reality, what happened was the market and the way the company had to compete in the market had gone through a fundamental transition. What had been valuable traits ten to fifteen years earlier and had served market conditions at that time were now obsolete, and I had not kept up with the market conditions. But when the day of reckoning came, it was easier for me to play the blame game and feel that I had been cheated, instead of understanding the dynamics that were at work and choosing to take full responsibility for what was happening in my career. It was a painful process, but I finally quit the blame game and took control of my career and my future prospects.

Does any of this sound familiar? Have you experienced it or seen it in someone in your family? It is actually a pretty common condition, but I have come to understand how foolish it was to think that way—and I now know that by using the context we are describing in this book and building a plan using the tools and techniques that are available, you will be more in control of your career and will not feel the need to blame.

VALUE SCANNING

When you play the blame game, you are a victim; your focus is on how you feel and on the entity that is doing you a disservice. That is not a productive way to operate and can only lead to more bitterness and frustration. As an alternative, you can drop the context of the blame game and actually embrace the idea of being constantly vigilant about opportunities that exist in the market. If you run a business, you are constantly looking out for the competition, for changes in the customer's needs, and for factors that will impact your profit margins. In I Incorporated, it is the same thing. You have to be aware of potential competition, potential customers, and opportunities to generate compensation.

Regarding the competition, be aware that there are people out there who are able to do what you do and do it faster, cheaper, or better. If you believe that no one else can do what you do, you are fooling yourself. Someone right now is in a garage developing something or some process that can do what you do for half the price and at twice the quality. Or someone with an advanced degree who is migrating from a foreign country today is hungry, wants your job, and is willing to do it for half what you make.

I am not saying this to make you paranoid or a protectionist. Free trade on a global basis provides us with a standard of living in the United States that is unheard of in many other parts of the world. The key is it needs to be "free." People have to be able to enter and exit the market freely in order for it to work. You can bury your head in the sand and hope it does not happen to you, or you can naïvely believe that your company will "take care of you," or you can get your antenna up, scan the horizon, understand your potential customers, evaluate your personal value proposition and constantly be able to clearly articulate the unique value you bring to the marketplace. If you can do that, you will be bulletproof, but if you cannot, you will wake up one morning with a pink slip and no idea how you are going to continue providing your family with the bare essentials. If you are in business for yourself, you must constantly look at the value of what you are providing. The same holds true in the world of I Incorporated.

How do you scan the horizon? How do you keep track of your value? How do you continuously monitor the value you bring and the demand for your services while you are busy doing your job? One thing you must understand is that scanning the horizon and knowing the value you bring to the market not only helps you, it also helps your current employer. If you have a better sense of your current value, you can continue to improve your contribution, and that will be good for you and your employer.

But let's go back to the business-plan concept to better understand how to scan the horizon. If you are in business for yourself, you must constantly look at the value of what you are providing. Are your customers' needs changing? Are there new competitors on the horizon? Is technology making your product or service less valuable or even obsolete? Business owners are constantly concerned with these factors. In order to remain in business, they must be vigilant, and as a result, the actions they take are not only good for their individual business, they are also good for the customer. And this is a key point! Business owners constantly look for ways to improve the product or service they are providing. This ensures that the customer continues to receive value and that the businessperson can stay in business.

The same thing applies to a career-acceleration plan. Remember that your employer is your client. Scanning the horizon and continuing to ensure that you are bringing value to your employer is good for you and for your employer. In fact, if you simply rely on the value that got you the position in the first place, you are going to become obsolete! There simply is too much change going on in the world for that obsolescence not to happen. You have to change. You have to remain current and relevant.

This is important for your career and will ensure you continue to bring value to your current employer, and to potential future employers, as opportunities present themselves. Constantly scan the horizon. Look for ways to continue bringing value, and you will be valuable to your current employer and able to take that new value proposition into the marketplace, if it becomes necessary to do so.

How do you go about scanning the horizon while you are busy working, going to college, or dealing with the myriad of other challenges we often find ourselves facing? This is where a lot of the career-planning tools can serve you. Regardless of where you live at this time, and if you have not done so already, get registered on LinkedIn, get a subscription to some current and relevant professional periodicals, and start reading the *Wall Street Journal* on a regular basis—all the while looking for opportunities to meet with people and learn about emerging opportunities. In addition, learn to have a specific purpose in mind when you do network.

Also, if you live in Michigan, I have included some additional resources later in this chapter under that heading. However, regardless of where you live, you can consult that list or simply reach out to your local librarian and ask them for help in researching potential companies and industries. You want to go beyond just what is in the local press or what is on their web page. It is fine to read that material but do a little more digging to truly find out how they operate, what their values are, how do they truly general revenue, what are their growth prospects and how viable are they for you to consider as a potential partner in your career pursuits.

MASS CUSTOMIZATION

I want to take a minute and share a genius marketing campaign with you. You may have gotten something similar on Facebook where there is an advertisement for a sweatshirt that has printed on the front where you were born "aka made" and where you currently live.

Initially I thought I was pretty special because here was a sweater that was targeted just for me with my home state proudly printed on the front along with where I currently live. And then when I went to order one, I realized that they probably did not even have them produced yet. But more importantly, they probably have sent this to just about everyone on Facebook that has listed where they grew up and where they currently live.

Talk about personalized attention! By taking advantage of some simple information, this entrepreneur is able to create a low-risk business venture, catering to the individual interests of each of us and doing it in a way that can create a smile on your face and make you a satisfied customer with very little initial investment.

This is clearly an example of taking advantage of the current environment and learning how to bring value to the market.

You might not be starting your own hoodie sweater business, but each of us need to be looking for ways to take advantage of the information that we have access to and learn to bring more value to the market as a result of the access we do have.

EVERYTHING IS CHANGING

You have probably heard of the expression, "planned obsolescence." Essentially it is the term used to describe the practice or policy of producing consumer goods that rapidly become obsolete and so that they require replacement, often by something that may have more functionality but may even be more expensive.

Everything becomes obsolete eventually. The jobs that our parents did have largely been enhanced or even replaced by technology. All you need to do is look around and see what some of the people in industry are currently doing, and you will see that many of these jobs did not even exist 10 or 15 years ago. That trend is going to continue, and even increase, so it is important for you to both understand that things are changing but also embrace the idea and take advantage of the opportunities that this fact provides to us.

On the flip side of planned obsolesce, is the idea of obsolescence that occurs simply as a by-product of a rapidly changing economy. We are calling this phenomenon, unplanned obsolescence. It is real and it continues to permeate all of our lives.

To get a feel for what I am talking about, go back 20 years or so and look at what the introduction of the personal computer and word processing software has done to typist and traditional secretary jobs. They have been virtually eliminated!

Another example that is more current is the explosion of GPS capabilities on your personal cell phone. Think about what GPS has done to producers of road atlases or specifically what it has done to the American Automobile Association by essentially replacing the service that they used to provide through their TripTik service. I can remember when we would take a long road trip and would have AAA produce a TripTiks to guide us along the way. Now my cell phone with the GPS provides even better trip management information with real time traffic updates and places to eat along the way.

Or what about the emergence of driverless cars. The technology is getting very close to being fully operational, and it will not be long before they are replacing long haul truckers with driverless technology. Driverless trucks do not need to take periodic rest stops and only need to stop for fuel as required. The impact may result in lower costs to transport goods as well as making them available more rapidly, but the impact on truck drivers and truck stop operators is going to be huge.

So the question is: What does this have to do with me? I am safe. I am not a typist, or a map maker or a truck driver. I know that no one can do my job as well as I can do it. Right?

Wrong! Look at what you do and assume that it can be replaced. The question is not: Can it be replaced? The question you need to ask is: How can it be replaced?

Now I am not saying this to make you paranoid or angry about "those immigrants" that are coming to America and taking jobs. And by the way, most everyone in the US is a result of immigration, so don't blame anyone. It is up to you to take control of your career and ensure that you do not become obsolete!

The worst thing you can do is to keep doing what you do under the mistaken belief that what served you last week will continue to be valuable next week.

So what can you do? It starts with accepting the fact that you must scrutinize what you do and ask yourself three fundamental question.

1. How can what I do be replaced by technology or by someone else who can do it for less money and/or higher quality? And don't think it cannot be done because it can be done.
2. Then, ask yourself if you truly want to stay in your current role.
3. If the answer is no, then get going on your new career quest and do not wait until you are replaced. However, if the answer is yes, then get started on re-engineering what you currently do so that you are truly bringing more value to the people you serve.

Look at what you are doing with a critical eye and imagine that you are paying someone else to do it. Ask if you feel that you are getting your money's worth? Figure out how to ensure that you are bringing value and then do what you need to do to change your approach so that it is more valuable.

And then, after you have done that, get ready to do it again. The point is that it never stops but as long as you are consistently looking at what you are doing and questioning the value of how you are currently doing it, you will be OK.

Realize that it is a never ending process, so get on board and do not allow for yourself to be a victim of "Unplanned Obsolescence." It can actually be a very exhilarating and positive experience. You might want to include some specific tasks in your career plan to test the "Unplanned Obsolescence" that might currently exist in your area of career interest, and develop a strategy to respond to what is happening in a positive and valuable way.

NETWORKING WITH A PURPOSE

What do we mean by "networking with a purpose"? We mean having a clear objective in mind whenever you engage with others in some form of networking environment. I heard once that while he was president, Lyndon Johnson would give his wife an assignment to find three people who could provide significant financial support to his campaign efforts every time she went to a networking event. You are probably not looking to run for president, but you do want to have a clear purpose in mind when you go to an event.

Some potential purposes might be:

1. Look for an opportunity to serve someone with a skill or ability that you are developing,
2. Find someone who can give you some practical advice about a certain career field,
3. Identify someone who can give you some specific insight into a certain industry, or
4. Connect with someone who would want to learn more about what you do.

Notice that I do not say to look for someone who is hiring. That is never the reason to network, even though it might be in the back of your mind. You network with people to make a connection, and the more you can have a specific agenda outside of finding out who is hiring, the better able you will be to connect with people who can serve you and whom you can also serve. When you go to an event, think about who is attending the event. Identify three or four key objectives for your participation and then ensure that you meet those objectives.

INFORMATIONAL INTERVIEWS

One key way to network with a purpose is to actually seek out what are called "informational interviews." Going on an informational interview does not mean you are looking to change jobs. In fact, doing an informational interview with someone in your current company can even be effective. After all, you are simply looking for information about how you can be more valuable in your current role. And when you think about it, this could be something that would be viewed positively by your current employer. After all, isn't it important to always know what it takes to be successful and then commit to a strategy to help enhance your current value to the workplace?

The key is that you are always in inquiry mode. You meet people on a plane, at a conference, through LinkedIn, or through a friend, and you look for opportunities to spend time with them to better understand the market, their sense of what is valuable, and what you can do to ensure that you bring value. You would do it if you were running your own business. There is no difference. Remember, you are in business for yourself, so networking whenever you have the opportunity has got to be good for your personal career-planning process.

That said, it is also a continuous process. In the following chapters, we will discuss some of the tools you need to master in the pursuit of your career aspirations, as well as dig deeper into the ideas of networking and informational interviews. We will also explore many specific tools such as an electronic portfolio. One thing that a portfolio can do is help you document examples of your personal value that you have developed in response to your value-scanning activities. Then, as your portfolio develops, you will want to keep it current by removing items that are becoming obsolete while adding examples of the new and emerging skills and abilities you have developed. You can also include examples of the track record you are continuing to develop that showcases the areas you have identified as being important as a result of your ongoing value-scanning activities.

However, before we get too entrenched in some of the tools, let's spend a little time with another concept that often gets ignored when people work on their career plans.

MARKETING

In order to develop this concept a little further, we must borrow a page from traditional marketing literature and see how it pertains both to starting a business and launching a career. We are talking about marketing, which is all about price, place, promotion, and product.

As an entrepreneur, you must develop a strategy to address all these elements, and as an individual developing your personal career-acceleration plan, you must do the same thing.

The Four P's of Marketing

FIGURE 3.1. THE FOUR P'S OF MARKETING.

THE FOUR P'S (LEVERS) OF MARKETING

The four P's of marketing theory are price, place, promotion, and product. In the business world they are relevant to how a company chooses to market its goods and services, and they are equally relevant to you in marketing your personal value. You can think about these as levers that you can pull to achieve the desired outcome. The better you are at pulling the right levers, the better you are going to be at achieving what you desire.

Price

Your own "price" is the value you feel you command in the market, and it comes from evaluation and analysis of compensation packages and salary surveys. We will talk more about negotiating a salary package later in the book, but for now you simply need to know that the price you choose to pursue is an integral part of your overall marketing strategy. In order to be successful, you must give it serious consideration, just like the other marketing factors. You bring value to the market, and you want to be able to think about that value in tangible terms.

Place

Your "place" is where you do the work. Most people assume they will go to work for a company and will be provided with a workspace at that firm. However, this is not always the case, and in many instances, you will be able to influence the decision.

Will you be in an office/work location, or will you work from home or on the road? Will you travel extensively or rely on technology to handle communication with people in different locations? You may also want to consider where your customer/client exists. Will you work in a central location and then travel to a client when you deliver your service? Do you need/want to be in an office or out making sales calls? Your definition of "place" can go a long way in articulating the value that you bring and is also an important factor in your consideration of what is important to you in your career.

Promotion

Your "promotion" strategy is all about how you brand yourself and then get the word out about what you can do through informational interviews and other networking opportunities. We will talk more about this in chapter 5, "Building Your Personal Brand," but it is important to realize that how you are promoted is a function of the effort and commitment that you put into the process. If you allow it to just happen, something will get promoted—but it might not be what you want it to be. The key is to know how you want to be perceived and then develop a strategy to consciously promote your brand in a purposeful way.

A successful entrepreneur will have a concerted focus on his or her promotion strategy, which often involves advertising campaigns, a focused presence in different social media sites, and other ways to get the word out to potential customers. You too must approach your career prospects from a similar perspective: Think about the story you want to tell and then choose the media and approach that will best serve your purpose.

Product

Lastly comes the "product," which is you. What are the skills, abilities, and experiences you have developed that define the product? How is the product unique? Who does the product appeal to? Why will someone want your product over someone else's? These are all key factors in an entrepreneurial venture and are equally important in a career development strategy.

These four factors are fundamental to any marketing strategy and will come up time and again in your personal career development process.

Let's continue to take a deeper dive into the world of an entrepreneur and see if there are more lessons to be learned in our career-planning process.

WHY COMPANIES FAIL

We all know that many small businesses fail, so it makes sense to understand some of those reasons and take action to guard against that happening in your career quest. The four main reasons they fail are as follows:

1. Inadequate market research
2. Limited financial support
3. Weak understanding of product/service
4. Insufficient stamina/drive to succeed

In order to maximize the probability of your success in your career quest, it is crucial that you consider these possible failure points seriously and develop a strategy to overcome them if possible.

IMPROVING YOUR MARKET RESEARCH

In order to help ensure success with your strategy, you must develop a strong sense of what the market will bear. The market for your services is what you must investigate. Look at the following: Who is doing the hiring? What are they looking for? What are the competitive pressures? All these factors are extremely important, and you must develop your own process for doing market research in your career-acceleration plan.

Some great ways to do this are through informational interviews and networking, and we will talk more about those specific approaches later in the book. Suffice it to say that in order to be successful, you absolutely must have a strong sense of the market and the potential value that you can bring to it. Commit to developing a sense of urgency to better understand your market and look for ways to support your research. And by the way, it takes work to figure this out, and you will always be looking for more information. Successful entrepreneurs know their market needs and are able to respond to those needs in a timely manner, but they are also constantly scanning the market for emerging opportunities.

Sometimes, entrepreneurs can identify what the market wants without even asking the market. Steve Jobs was famous for envisioning what people wanted without asking them. In fact, even if he had asked, how could people have told him they wanted an iPad? He led the market, and you can do the same thing. Anticipate what the need is. Don't wait for someone to tell you. If you do, you may be too late. Give it some serious thought, envision how you can add value, and then develop your plan ahead of the competition.

FINANCIAL BACKING

In the next chapter, we will discuss the idea of surviving, adapting, and ultimately flourishing in your career quest. It is important you are able to maintain your livelihood while you are on this quest. I once had a colleague suggest I get a job at a local hardware store while I was in the job-search process. My initial reaction was that I was appalled. How could I look myself in the mirror if I was performing a job for close to minimum wage when I had previously had a job in the low six-figure range? However, I finally came to the realization that I needed to get over myself. A job that provided some financial support while I was on my quest for my career opportunity was not a bad idea. In fact, it is what I eventually wound up doing, but initially it was a tough pill to swallow.

It is obviously important that you have some financial resources to get you through the tough spots. If this means working at an entry-level job to help tide you over, then that is what you must do. The key point is you must be prepared to do what you must and be willing to put up with some hardships in the short run, as long as you can keep your eye on the goal.

PRODUCT/SERVICE KNOWLEDGE

An entrepreneur must fully know what his or her product/service is capable of performing and what adjustments might be possible in order to take advantage of market conditions not originally considered. In fact, there is a concept called "features and benefits" that I want to introduce at this time.

A product's features are what you can see when you look at the product. Is it red or green? Is it made out of steel or aluminum? Features are relatively easy to identify, and they influence the purchase of the item to some degree. In your case features might be things like having a college degree, being certified in project management, or even having five years' experience in a given role. These features will help you in the job quest, but they are only part of the story.

A product's benefits are what the consumer derives from using the product. You may want to buy a red car, so the feature of a red car will help you narrow down the choices, but the final decision will be a red car that gives you the benefits that you desire. There will be many red cars to choose from, but the one with the best gas mileage, safety rating, or maintenance history will get your attention. You must decide what your features are and how you can use them to differentiate you in the marketplace. We will talk more about this idea in chapter 7, "Articulating Your Personal Value Proposition," but for now, just know that you must understand both your personal features and benefits in order to effectively market yourself in today's economy.

You can look around and see all sorts of products that have been adjusted as the demand for different attributes has changed. The most glaring is the smart phone. To call it a "phone" today is a bit of a misnomer. It is a portable computer that can fully connect to the internet and can be used to call people, take pictures, find out where you are, and even play music. In only a few years, the phone has morphed into a totally different piece of equipment to respond to consumer interests and demands.

You must also be able to rise to the challenge. When you look at your current features and benefits, they may be good for today, but it will not take long for them to become obsolete. You must continually reinvent yourself and your abilities in order to continue to secure viable opportunities in the marketplace. An entrepreneur who allows his product/service to become stale will soon find him- or herself out of business. Once again, the same holds true for you and your career development.

DRIVE

Any book you pick up about a successful entrepreneur will tell you about that person's unquenchable drive to succeed. Every time successful entrepreneurs hit a roadblock, they figure out a way around it. Nothing, absolutely nothing, will stop them from achieving their goals. These roadblocks include external factors, competition, delays in the shipment of parts, family members, or their own nagging concerns that what they are doing will fail. Any and all of these factors come to play a part in the downfall of many entrepreneurs' visions for success. However, the strong prevail and continue to make their business ventures successful, but the weak and timid quickly give in to the enormous pressures.

Walt Disney even had a bit of a rough start. He was fired by a newspaper editor because "he lacked imagination and had no good ideas."

Don't ever let anybody tell you that you do not have what it takes to be successful. However, you must develop a strong drive and accept the fact that you may fail many times along the way. Do not even enter into this approach if you are looking for an easy way to get a quick job. Anything worth having is worth working for, and if you want a challenging, viable, and rewarding career that is worthy of you, you must be prepared to overcome resistance and channel your drive and energy toward accomplishing your goal.

That does not mean that it is drudgery or a terrible experience to pursue your career aspirations. Actually, it is very much the opposite. Pursuit of your true career aspirations is a noble venture. It is empowering, engaging, and a feat worthy of your effort. Find your dream, strive to achieve it, and never let the naysayers tell you it will not work. Stick to your commitments, and you will be rewarded in the long run. I have been, and I know it works.

The most significant similarity between starting a business and a career comes down to the level of commitment you have for the objective. Nothing we have talked about or will cover in this book is easy. You have to be prepared to work at it. It is not unheard of to think of a career quest being a full-time job. Launching a business is all-consuming, and launching your career can require just as much of a commitment.

However, the benefits are worth the effort. Just like a budding entrepreneur, you must network. Learn your elevator speech and practice it again and again. Be prepared to tell your personal story effectively and with passion. Show commitment to your objectives, stick to your convictions, and have faith in the outcome. It does work for entrepreneurs, and it will work for you.

ADDITIONAL RESOURCES

Here are some suggested ideas for you to gain further information about potential companies if you are living in Michigan. Take advantage of the free databases available through the Michigan Electronic Library (MeL). Begin at your local public library's website and look for the MeL link. From there, you will be able to access business database such as:

- Academic OneFile
- Business Decision
- Business Insights: Global
- General OneFile

Narrow your search to business news and choose a date range that is current. You can even specify a specific source if you wish (i.e. Harvard Business Review, MIT Sloan Management Review, etc.)

In addition to this content, if you are a student within the University of Michigan system, you can use the Mardigian Library's subscription to the Factiva database to access top *Wall Street Journal* articles each day of the week. You can also use Browzine, an online browsing service, available through the Mardigian Library, to read new issues of hundreds of magazines as they are released or even create an online bookshelf. And lastly, you can browse the Business Section of the *Detroit Free Press* (www.freep.com) and *Crain's Detroit Business* (www.crainsdetroit.com) for local and regional business news.

NOW WHAT?

How can you practice some of these ideas? One thing to consider is that most learning happens through doing, not just reading about a topic or listening to a lecture. The idea of the "Now What?" sections in this book is to give you the chance to experience, firsthand, how you can apply these concepts.

Here are some suggestions, and you might want to commit to one or two, document them in your career plan, commit to when you will do them and then give yourself a pat on the back when you actually complete the task. None of what we are discussing in this book is easy. It takes effort and commitment to make this a reality. However, the benefits of embracing and pursuing these ideas will help you throughout your professional career. Take some time, give it some thought, commit to results and make it happen. You can:

1. Meet with some true entrepreneurs, and do not limit yourself just to the ones who have been successful. You will learn a lot from those who have failed but have not quit. Take them out for coffee and learn what they have done in order to be successful or what they have learned from their failures. However, remember you are not trying to start your own business. Just listen to what they have been through and then translate that into your own world to see if there is a way to apply it to your job search.
2. Read a book or two about entrepreneurship, such as *The Entrepreneurial Mindset* by Rita Gunther McGrath and Ian MacMillan or *The Start-Up of You* by Reid Hoffman and Ben Casnocha.
3. Attend a conference or seminar on entrepreneurship at your school or local chamber of commerce.
4. Go to a networking event that is likely to draw entrepreneurs and do some purposeful networking.
5. Start a journal, and as you gain more exposure to entrepreneurial concepts, write down your thoughts and feelings and what you might be able to do to take even further advantage of the opportunities.
6. Talk over the ideas in this chapter with your friends and colleagues. Challenge them to think with an entrepreneurial mind-set and help them discover how they can be more empowered by embracing this concept.

Remember, the idea is for you to challenge your current way of thinking so that it is more entrepreneurial. You do not need to be thinking about starting your own business, but you do need to be thinking about how you market yourself as if you were your own business. Take some time to learn from others who have mastered the concept and then strive to apply it to your own view of the world.

And be sure to dig out your individual career plan and make some specific commitments to help you become more entrepreneurial, aka empowered, in the pursuit of your career aspirations. This will definitely take more effort than simply sending your resume out to some job postings, but if you make the commitment to develop and then execute on the plan, it will pay you dividends now and for the rest of your professional life.

REFERENCES

Bilanich, Bud. "50 Famous People Who Failed at Their First Attempt at Career Success." *Bud Bilanich* (blog). http://www.budbilanich.com/50-famous-people-who-failed-at-their-first-attempt-at-career-success.

Bolles, Richard N. *What Color Is Your Parachute? A Practical Manual for Job-Hunters and Career-Changers*. New York: Random House, 2013.

CitiGroup, So you want to be an Entrepreneur, http://*www.citigroup.com/citi/citizen/community/data/guide1_eng.pdf*

Hoffman, Reid, and Ben Casnocha. *The Start-Up of You: Adapt to the Future, Invest in Yourself, and Transform Your Career*. New York: Crown Business, 2012.

Jobs, Steven. *https://www.entrepreneur.com/slideshow/233085*

McGrath, Rita Gunther, and Ian MacMillan. *The Entrepreneurial Mindset*. Boston, MA: Harvard Business School Press, 2000.

Peters, Tom. *Thriving on Chaos: A Handbook for a Management Revolution*. New York: Harper Collins, 1987.

Pink, Daniel H. *Free Agent Nation: The Future of Working for Yourself*. New York: Warner Business, 2001.

4

Surviving the Rough Spots

WHY WE USE THE IDEA OF SURVIVE, ADAPT, AND FLOURISH

The idea of survive, adapt, and flourish comes from observing successful business leaders in a variety of roles. We all have times when things do not go as we had planned. Songs are written and sung about overcoming challenges, people who effectively deal with adversity are often immortalized, and we are consistently inspired by

FIGURE 4.1. DEALING WITH ADVERSITY.

people who continue to persevere. The survive, adapt, and flourish (SAF) mind-set can help you create and maintain a context that will help you through these challenges.

It is entirely possible that you will find opportunities that are exciting and fit well with your personal values, or that you have even begun to develop a track record that would support your being considered for a position in your chosen field. However, you may also be coming up short in a few different areas. If that is the case, then what should you do?

There is definitely a recurring theme that comes across every time you speak with successful entrepreneurs: They probably were not successful right out of the gate. They tried something, failed, made some adjustments, tried again, and kept at it until it was successful. Even Henry Ford failed five times in his attempts to start a business until he hit it big and started Ford Motor Company. Thomas Edison failed 1,000 times before he got the lightbulb correct, and Colonel Sanders of Kentucky Fried Chicken had his famous secret recipe rejected 1,009 times before a restaurant accepted it. The list goes on.

I could sit here and tell you to persevere and never give up, which is good advice but borders on being trivial. Everyone tells you the same thing, and it does make sense to never give up. But I want to take it a little deeper and give you a context that will help you through the journey.

MAKING CHOICES

There are several estimates out there about how many choices we make on an average day, but some folks argue that it is probably close to over 30,000 individual decisions each day. We are constantly making choices. We decide what food to eat, what to wear, how to go to work, or go home, or even to decide if we want to go to work today. Literally thousands of times we can choose what we want to do and then experience the outcome.

So why is this important? After all, aren't most of our decisions actually made for us, and we just choose to follow them? Some people would make that argument and would then claim that we have very little control over what happens in our lives. An alternative perspective, and one that we subscribe to in this book, is that we are in control, we have the power to choose and we should take time to consciously think about the possible outcomes as often as we can.

Now, I fully realize that we cannot stop and think every time we make a decision. Some decisions are made by instinct, but many of those are the result of prior experiences and training. Think about when you are driving and how your instincts kick in when someone pulls out in front of you. You know exactly what to do but it took some experience to get to that point.

Taking the driving example a little further, imagine how competent you are as a driver and then think about what would happen if you were instantly transported to a different country where they drive on the other side of the road. All bets are off! Everything changes and all of those familiar instincts are challenged because you cannot rely on them as easily as before.

I would argue that the current job market can often be similar to driving in a different country. What served you in the past may no longer serve you going forward. Your assumptions about company values, or job security, or even governmental regulations are all subject to change.

The main point is to accept the fact that you are making thousands of choices each day. It is important that you realize that and never get lulled into the belief that what served you in the past will continue to get you the desired outcomes. Understand your choices, pay attention to them, constantly be alert for changes that you need to make and accept that you are largely accountable for the outcomes of the choices that we do make.

DEALING WITH THE CONSEQUENCES

I realize that most students have already been exposed to this fairly simple idea, but since it is so important within the realm of career planning and development, it bears repeating one more time.

"I believe that we are solely responsible for our choices, and we have to accept the consequences of every deed, word, and thought throughout our lifetime." —Elisabeth Kubler-Ross

Elisabeth Kubler-Ross was an American born psychologist who wrote extensively about choices and the consequences we face as a result of those choices.

She warned us about what can happen if you are not aware of the fact that your behavior has consequences. For instance: when the results are negative, you run the risk of repeating the behavior and, hence, suffering the same consequence. If the results are positive, you mail fail to duplicate the behavior and, as a result, wind up being frustrated.

The idea that I want to recommend is to take a moment to reflect on something that has happened to you recently, either positive or negative. When you think about what happened, is your tendency to explain it in terms of what someone else did? For instance, when you get a poor, or good, grade on an exam, is it ever the professor's fault? Was the test too hard, or too easy?

It is so easy for us to fall into the trap of trying to "fix" someone else. The truth is that you cannot "fix" the problem in someone else. It is crucial for you to think about the outcome, decide what you can do to influence future outcomes, change or reinforce your behavior accordingly and then bear the fruits from the desired behavior.

Your career prospects are a function of your behavior. If you have multiple opportunities that you want to pursue, that is a consequence of prior behaviors. If you are striking out and not making any connections, that too is a consequence of your prior behaviors. It is not because of the school you attended, or a specific instructor or some other external driver. It is your career and you own the outcome. No one else owns it. Others will certainly influence it, but it is yours and yours alone. Accept responsibility for the consequences and prepare to move on.

SAILING AS A POWERFUL METAPHOR

One way to visualize this idea can be found in watching a high-powered professional sailing regatta. When you have an opportunity, tune into an "America's Cup" race or some other sailing event that is truly challenging to crew and equipment on the boats that are competing.

If you have never had the privilege of sailing in, or even observing, one of these races, I am sure that if you watch the condition of the boats, especially when they are sailing into the wind, it is easy to imagine how you might think that they are ready to tip over and lose everyone on board. The boats are often keeled over at a very sharp angle and they truly look very precarious.

However, the fact is that they are often completely under control. In fact, these boats are designed to operate under those types of conditions, just like you and I are designed to operate "under sail." It is sometimes frightening to venture out of your comfort zone and it can feel much safer to remain in the dock, but the rewards are there for those who are willing to learn how to "sail" and then embrace the wind.

Now, I know I might be overdoing it a little with the sailing metaphor, but it truly is a powerful image for you to use when you think about the possible changes you might be wanting to take in your career pursuits. Just like the America Cup sailors, you will need to practice, to explore possible options and strategies, and yes, fail occasionally. But if you accept responsibility for the outcomes, evaluate your behaviors as you experience different consequences, and stay focused on the desired outcomes, you too will become a skilled and proficient sailor in your own right.

SURVIVE, ADAPT, AND FLOURISH DEFINED

Throughout all of these experiences whether you are dealing with challenge and change, getting outside of your comfort zone, or simply trying a new way to drive to school or work, there are three recurring themes that continue to show up when we look at people who have gotten through adversity. These themes will continue to present themselves time and again as you work through the career-planning process. Again, don't forget you want to embrace the entrepreneurial mind-set and that entrepreneurs go through this cycle time and time again.

These three themes will repeat themselves over and over again throughout the process. It is as if they are the guiding mantra beneath all this effort and are totally in line with the idea of an entrepreneurial mentality. Specifically, there are three phases to the cycle. They are:

SURVIVE

Take care of yourself. Be sure you have plans in place to pay the bills. You might even need to take a position beneath your current expectations in the short run to keep the bill collectors away. Also, you may want to engage in volunteer work that will keep you engaged in the workplace while continuing to build your track record and your relationships, as well as help you keep a good outlook about the future.

You have to survive, and you have to do so in a way that does not damage your health, your reputation, or the people in your life that are important. Survive! Have short-term goals that get you through the rough times.

ADAPT

As you are taking care of business and surviving the process, you also want to be able to embrace and adapt to changing circumstances.

You may have found yourself unemployed because of global competition, or you may be just entering the workforce and are not sure what your key value proposition is. The point of this phase is that you may have to adapt in order to pursue a viable career. In fact, this type of adaptation may be necessary throughout your entire professional life.

There are few opportunities in life that remain static. Most positions or areas of interest are constantly changing. New technologies are making the old ways of doing things obsolete. Global competition is constantly creating the pressure to change how companies are doing things. The key thought here is that you must prepare to adapt to the changing environment. Do not try to resist it, but rather embrace it.

Also, adapting to the changes will be much easier if you have developed a short-term survival strategy. However, if you do not take care of the survival issues, you will find it difficult to adapt because you will be in a resistance mindset. Entrepreneurs adapt all the time. It is what keeps them viable, and you too must be willing to constantly adapt to changes in the marketplace. Embrace the concept, set your midrange goals to align with ways to adapt, and then embrace what is happening around you.

FLOURISH

This is what makes it all worthwhile. Embrace the idea that ultimately, you will flourish. An entrepreneur knows that he or she will be successful. It will happen. The world is an abundant place.

Regardless of your background, education, and experience, you can flourish. You must believe this, and you must be able to step into the opportunity when it presents itself.

There are a multitude of motivational speakers who talk about having a positive self-image, managing your thoughts in a positive manner, or always having an upbeat attitude. These ideas are relevant and important for you to embrace in this phase. Have faith in your ability, and the outcomes will present themselves.

There is an expression that goes like this: "When the student is ready, the teacher will appear." That is what this phase is all about. You have to be ready. You have to take care of the basics and ensure that you are surviving in a positive manner. You have to embrace the concept that you must adapt, and you must put processes and goals in place to help you do just that.

As you ensure that you survive and adapt, you will then be more open to allow positive opportunities to flow into your life and to know that you will flourish, just like any successful entrepreneur will do.

VALLEY OF DESPAIR

I was originally introduced to the concept of the "valley of despair" when I was prepared to move to a foreign country. People told me all about the idea, but I failed to believe it was true. Then, after my family and I had been in country for a few months, the valley of despair truly set in and I had to deal with a fairly high degree of anxiety and frustration.

Now, the term "despair" might be a little too strong, and it is possible that you will never experience it at that level of anxiety, but it can be very destabilizing and cause some fairly consistent anxiety.

WHAT IS IT?

So what is the valley of despair? Take a look at the following graphic. The idea is that whenever you choose to make a change in your life of any significant consequence, you may experience an initial period of euphoria. When you move to a different country, this is the time when you are running around with your camera, enjoying the new scenery and trying to take advantage of the new

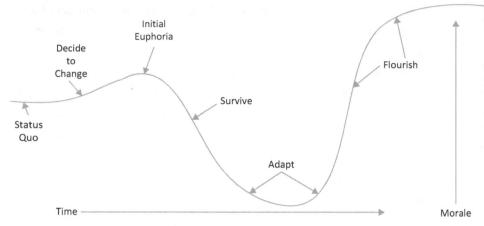

FIGURE 4.2. VALLEY OF DESPAIR

opportunities. You are happy with your choice and are trying to embrace all of the new stimuli. A new job, a new city, even a new relationship can all result in this initial euphoric sense.

THE PHASES OF THE VALLEY OF DESPAIR

Shortly after the euphoric time, "reality" sets in. You start comparing your new environment to your prior one. This is where people who are new to a job keep saying how it was back where they were and how much better it was at that time. There can often be a fairly profound sense of loss or frustration during this time. To say that you are depressed is fairly minor compared to some of the dysfunctional things that can happen. It can be very painful, and it is important that you have some kind of support system to help you through this period. In our vernacular, we call this the "survive" phase.

After a period of time, you learn to adapt to the new environment. If you are in a different country, this is where you start learning the language or customs of the new country. If it is a new job, you are learning the new processes and procedures. The important part of this phase is that you are willing to let go of the past, and embrace the new environment as not different from the past but rather simply a different way of being. Not good or bad, just different and you do not need to compare it to the past.

This is where the maximum opportunity exists. During the "survive" phase, you are simply trying to survive. It is hard to focus on much of anything else other than getting through the day and keeping your performance where it needs to be. However, once you move into the "adapt" phase, you are now ready to be open to new opportunities and take advantage of them when they come along.

The last phase is where you get to reap the rewards of the fact that you made the decision and chose to jump into the valley of despair. This is where you can truly "flourish" as a result of what you have learned and been able to absorb through the "adapt" phase. This is why it makes sense to embark on a path the can lead you to the valley of despair. We will talk a little more about the idea of "flourish" in the next section, but for now, I want you to embrace two beliefs. The first is that the valley truly does exist, and the second is that you will go through it many times in your life. When you are in it, it does not mean that you are a failure or made a bad decision. It is real, it happens to all of us, and so the challenge is not to avoid it, but rather embrace it and pursue strategies that will shorten the duration and the depth so that you can move through it more quickly.

WHY WOULD I EVER WANT TO ENTER IT?

This really is a good question, and I would never recommend that you make the decision to enter the valley in a casual manner. Getting yourself into a situation that can result is some fairly significant anxiety may not always be a good idea.

On the other hand, you will need to embrace some paths that will qualify as falling into the valley of despair. The key is to choose wisely. Embrace those challenges that you feel are worth your time and efforts and that you believe you will be able to accommodate. However, be prepared to stretch yourself a little. "One does not discover new lands without consenting to lose sight of the shore for a very long time." —Andre Gide.

HOW DO I RECOGNIZE IT?

The first place to look is to be sensitive to your personal feelings. When you go through a personal change, be sure to take time to reflect, be quiet and listen to what your instincts are telling you. When you give voice to these instincts and allow them to be present, you not only can better understand what is happening but also are much better prepared to deal with it.

Let's imagine that you have decided to try a different major in college. Your friends seem to be much happier or you believe that the job prospects are better or you just wanted to try something different. Regardless of the driving force behind it, a change of this nature may definitely take you through the valley of despair, and if you are not paying attention, the anxiety may become significant and will be what you are focusing on, instead of what is truly happening and how you can deal with it.

Almost any change of any significant consequence is going to take you through the valley. Pay attention to your health and mental attitude. Try to maintain your focus. Keep in touch with your friends, and know that "this too will pass."

The key is to simply acknowledge that it is happening and then, once you have done that, you can figure out the best way to deal with it.

HOW CAN I DEAL WITH IT?

There are a variety of ways to deal with the valley of despair, and depending on the depth and anticipated duration, you will probably want to choose different strategies. Deciding to drive a different way to school or work may cause a minor valley that will probably only last for one trip, so it would be silly to try to change your behavior as a result of that decision.

However, anything that causes a significant rise in your anxiety level and something that is lasts more than a day or two, deserves some attention. The following list of suggestions can help you either prepare for or actually weather the valley as you are experiencing it. Needless to say, the more prepared you are before you enter the valley, the easier it will be to shorten the duration and/or the depth of your personal valley.

Here are some possible suggestions to help you weather the storm and get to the point where you can ultimately flourish as a result of your choice

ELEVATOR PITCH

The idea of an elevator pitch is simple. We all meet many different people in our daily routines, and we certainly do not have the luxury of spending 10–15 minutes with them to help them get to know us and our dreams and aspirations. At best, we have a few brief moments, maybe as long as it takes to ride down in an elevator, to tell someone the key things that you want them to know about you.

There are two ways to go about developing your elevator pitch. The first is to focus on who you are. If you take this approach you are going to focus on the fact that you are, or were, a college student with a specific major, or that you are currently working at a local company, or that you are enjoying watching a specific sports team and you might mention that you are currently looking for a job.

Now, put yourself in the shoes of someone listening to this pitch. Are you impressed? More importantly, do you really care about what you are hearing, and can it have any value to you? I know it can sound pretty self-serving, but people want to know, "What's in it for me?" When they are listening to you talk they are thinking about what impact it might have on them or their business. If the impact is neutral, they will smile, pay attention until the elevator doors open and then say goodbye and wish you good luck in your future pursuits.

The second option is to think about the key areas where you can bring value to a company. It might be that you are a great project manager, or technical analyst, or problem solver, or computer programmer or even a very strong marketer. Think about what those key elements are and then be prepared to discuss them when you have the opportunity, i.e. meet an executive in an elevator.

When you do that and take the chance to talk with someone, you can introduce yourself and maybe mention where you go, or went, to college but quickly get the other person talking about what they do and the challenges they have in their job. If you can get them to open up just a little, then you have the opportunity to talk about the value that you can bring to that problem building on the key values that you have already identified.

This is not easy. It is much safer to simply talk about where you go to school, what you are studying and how badly you want to work for a good company, but that approach will not get you very far in today's job market. However, when you are able to frame what you can do and the value you can bring to a given organization that will address real needs, the more powerful you will feel and the better able you will be to move through your valley of despair and continue your career quest.

We will be talking a lot more about networking and how to get someone to open up to you, but the key is to think about the value you bring to the job market, be proud of that value, know that it will serve you well and look for opportunities to share it with someone. Just like when you are taking an exam and you are well prepared, you want to bring it on and do a good job. Be prepared for the elevator pitch opportunity. Know the value that you can bring, and look for the opportunity to present yourself. When you have that attitude working for you, you will be much more confident and your ability to deal with anxiety and change in your life will be greatly enhanced.

SMART GOALS

Another technique to help you through the valley of despair is to set and track your progress against your goals. It is extremely important in implementing a SAF strategy that will serve you in your career quest. In order to make it easier, there is actually a formula for defining an effective goal, and it follows the acronym *SMART*.

Specifically, *SMART* goals are:

<u>S</u>pecific, <u>M</u>easurable, <u>A</u>ttainable, <u>R</u>elevant, and <u>T</u>ime Based

At the end of this book, we will review the idea of creating a viable career-acceleration plan that will help guide you in coming the months and years. That plan requires that you establish goals, both in the short term and over a longer duration. These goals can help you with the SAF strategy, but it is important that you evaluate them in accordance with the SMART strategy.

For instance, a specific goal would be to attend two entrepreneurial seminars in the next three months, whereas a nonspecific goal would be to attend some seminars about entrepreneurship. The second one is OK, but the first is tangible and you can measure your progress against it.

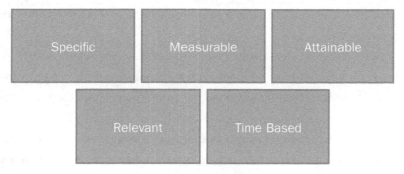

FIGURE 4.3. ELEMENTS CONTAINED IN SMART GOALS.

A measurable goal would be to contact three friends and ask them for input on your personal brand, whereas a less measurable goal would be to talk to some people about your brand. You can measure the first, but you cannot measure the second.

An attainable goal is something that is realistic for you to accomplish. It can have a stretch element, but if it is too big a challenge, it probably will not get done. An attainable goal would be to ask five people what they feel is most important to their careers, whereas an unattainable goal would be to ask everyone in your family what is important to their careers.

Relevant goals are extremely important. You might have a goal to talk to a professor about his or her career, but you must consider how relevant that would be. If you intend to seek out a career as a professor, it would be very relevant, but if you plan to go into the business world, it may not be quite as relevant. Obviously, it depends on what you want to accomplish, but try not to take the easy road and contact only people who are readily accessible.

Lastly, you want to consider the time commitment of your goals. This is often the part that gets forgotten because in order to state when you will have the goal completed, you must make the personal commitment that you will, in fact, do it. The idea is to say what you plan to do and then do what you say. Most leaders will confirm that that mantra is extremely valuable to follow, and it starts with establishing a goal that has a clear time frame. For instance, a timely goal would be something like: participate in three mock interviews by October 15 of this year.

A less timely goal would be something like: participate in three mock interviews as soon as I can.

Draw a line in the sand and make the personal commitment so that you know when your goals are due, and you will be able both to measure their attainment and to celebrate when you have met them within the stated time frame.

Take some time to set up your goals using this structure for all three sections of the SAF timeline. It is ultimately up to you, but if you follow this approach, you will take care of your immediate needs, ensure that you are open to a rapidly changing world, and prepare yourself to embrace the abundant opportunities that will come into your life.

KNOW YOUR VALUE

We will go into more detail about actual salary negotiation in chapter 11, but there are some key factors that bear consideration at this time. In helping you deal with some of anxiety associated with making a significant change, it is good to get an idea of your value in the marketplace as a result of the decision that you have made.

This is where a lot of people can get themselves into a quandary. They may have decided to make a change in their lives, are going through their personal valley of despair, and are hoping that it will be worth the effort that they have decided to take on. The key is that if you are simply hoping it will lead to a better financial situation, you may be setting yourself up for failure. On the other hand, if you do your research, know what the compensation ranges are from a reliable source and that are consistent with your anticipated new role, you will be much better able to weather the storm. Nothing will make you more comfortable and able to get through the valley more quickly than knowing the facts. Hoping something will happen or that you will gain a better financial situation will only go so far.

The mistake most people make is that they consider their potential value and corresponding compensation in terms of either something they want, something they need or something they deserve. The first two may be very real and you should have needs and wants, but when it comes to justification for a given level of compensation, what you deserve is the only one that is relevant.

It is up to you to take the time to do your research. Understand what they market will truly pay for someone with that new set of skills and abilities and use that factual data to help you get through the valley and on into the phase where you can truly flourish as a result of the change that you had made.

STRIVE FOR FINANCIAL SECURITY

In addition to doing your research and knowing how the job market will value your new skills and abilities, you might also want to take it one step further and do some research and planning to help with your overall financial security.

We all know that way too many college students are graduating with a huge financial burden of having to repay loans that were necessary to get through college. Now, it would be easy for me to say to not borrow the money, but I know that that is not always feasible. However, you want to have a plan. If you do need to go into debt, have a re-payment plan in place before your graduate. Know what you are worth and set your sights on that kind of salary, but on top of that, do some research about personal financial management.

It is obviously beyond this book to provide a comprehensive overview of personal financial planning, but one resource you might want to check out is a course provided by Dave Ramsey. There is a 5-week version and a 12-week version of his course. It is fairly inexpensive and something that might be worth your time and effort. I will include the reference data in the "Additional Resources" section of this chapter.

Regardless of where you get it, increase your understanding of personal financial management. There are some basics regarding how to set up checking and savings accounts, getting life insurance and making sure that you are protected in the short run. Also, you need to understand the time value of money, how to make sound investments and how not to be burdened by an overwhelming amount of debt for many years after graduation. This kind of planning can also help you get through your valley more quickly and be much more confident in the ultimate outcome of your personal decisions.

ADDITIONAL RESOURCES

There are basically two kinds of salary surveys out there for you to access. The more public ones, like the NY Times/Glassdoor option, are developed from surveys of job incumbents. Since it is relying on people to actually be truthful in their reporting, some people feel that it might be slightly inflated. You can access it at: https://www.glassdoor.com/Salary/New-York-Times-Salaries-E960.htm

Conversely, you can access salary surveys that are built from information that companies provide. This data is often more accurate, but you may have to pay a subscription fee. One of the most common surveys of this type is produced through the National Association of Colleges and Employers (NACE). You can certainly access it through the following site: http://www.naceweb.org/salary-survey-data/ and order it, or you can simply work with your local career services organization that probably has access to this data.

I recommend that you take a look at the *New York Times* data to get a feel for your compensation range and then, when it is time to be getting closer to actual salary negotiations, you might want to seek out a copy of the NACE Salary Survey report.

A second resource that you might want to investigate regarding your personal financial management is the Dave Ramsey material. You can locate it at the following website: https://www.daveramsey.com/fpu

There are a multitude of potential programs to help you gain a stronger understanding of your personal financial situation. Visit the web page, review the programs and look for what will serve you best given your current situation. I think you will be happy with what you find, and it will be well worth your time to invest in one of the programs.

A third resource that might be valuable to consult when you hit a bump in the road is provided by the *Harvard Business Review* and can be found at the following website: https://hbr.org/2016/12/5-steps-to-help-yourself-recover-from-a-setback. It will offer you a 5-step process to help review what happened, the choices you made along with way and how you might be able to create a different outcome.

Lastly, if you want to get a better idea of cognitive behavioral therapy, you could take a look at the following website: https://en.wikipedia.org/wiki/

Cognitive_behavioral_therapy. The whole idea of systematically changing your behaviors, your feelings and your thoughts can take you a long way to achieving different outcomes, and the theory behind this approach can be very valuable.

Regardless of which options you choose to explore, give it some further thought, research these and others and take some time to truly change where it can serve you better. The valley of despair is real and can cause some major personal issues, but it can be managed, and there are a wealth of options available to you. Good luck in your quest!

NOW WHAT?

Of all the concepts we cover in this book, the paradigm involving survive, adapt, and flourish is often the most difficult to apply. However, instead of just trying to identify how you can survive, adapt, and flourish, maybe the best strategy is simply to learn how to think different. I use the word *different* instead of *differently* because I am borrowing a page from Steve Jobs. He challenged his team to think different, and I am challenging you to do the same in this case. Learn to think different, especially when it comes to these three concepts. Here are some suggestions of ways you can learn to think different when it comes to your career.

1. Get on YouTube and watch some sailing regattas. Pay attention to what the boats and the crews do when they are under stress and think about how you can learn from their behaviors and channel them into some of the actions you can take with regard to your personal career.
2. Do some reading outside of your traditional space. Read about history, philosophy, the arts, literature, or anything else that will help you challenge your current paradigm.
3. Watch some of the shows on the History Channel and think about how people applied the concept of survive, adapt, and flourish in their lives. Think about their experiences and how they weathered their own valley of despair. Observe what worked and possibly what did not work for them and if you have the opportunity, discuss what you observe with friends or family and how you might be able to apply some of those concepts in your personal life.

4. Begin a journal. Take time each day to write down some of your key experiences, and then periodically go back and review it. Look for the trends. See what has happened in your life regarding how you have applied the concepts already, and then continue to do so going forward.

5. Find one or more people who have been through a challenging ordeal and ask them to tell you their story. Listen carefully for examples of what they did to survive, how they chose to adapt, and how they have ultimately moved into a realm of flourishing.

The fundamental idea is that you will need to draw upon these types of skills in the future. The more you have read about possible scenarios or talked with people who have been through ordeals, the more likely you will be successful when you are confronted with similar challenges.

Maybe you can also come up with some possible ideas on how to practice strengthening your ability to survive, adapt, and flourish.

My challenge to you is to take some time and expand your current way of thinking to be more in touch with the larger system within which we all operate. Learn how to allow things to unfold for you. It can be challenging and even potentially depressing sometimes, but prepare yourself and strive to be open to the possibilities! The universe is an abundant place.

And take some time to enter some specific steps that you plan to take in your personal career plan. The idea is to anticipate and prepare. Think about specific things that you can do to both prepare you for potential "Valleys of Despair" but also to help you get through them more quickly and with less personal disruption when the do occur.

REFERENCES

Bilanich, Bud. "*50 Famous People Who Failed at Their First Attempt at Career Success.*" *Bud Bilanich* (blog). http://www.budbilanich.com/50-famous-people-who-failed-at-their-first-attempt-at-career-success.

Gide, Andre, Brainy Quotes https://www.brainyquote.com/quotes/quotes/a/andregide108334.html

Isaacson, Walter. *Steve Jobs*. New York: Simon & Schuster, 2011.

Harvard Business Review, *Steps to help you recover from a setback* https://hbr. org/2016/12/5-steps-to-help-yourself-recover-from-a-setback

Kubler-Ross, Elisabeth, *Brainy Quotes* https://www.brainyquote.com/quotes/ quotes/e/elisabethk121108.html

NACE *Salary Survey* http://www.naceweb.org/salary-survey-data/

Quora, *How many decisions does a person make in an average day* https://www. quora.com/How-many-decisions-does-a-person-make-in-an-average-day

Ramsey, Dave, *You can take control of your money* https://www.daveramsey.com/ fpu

Simoes, Jorge *The Valley of Despair* https://betterleadership.wordpress.com/ 2010/02/05/the-valley-of-despair/

Wikipedia, *Cognitive Behavioral Therapy* https://en.wikipedia.org/wiki/Cognitive_ behavioral_therapy

SECTION 3.
DISCOVERING the OPPORTUNITIES

INTRODUCTION

W e now shift our focus away from looking at our personal mind-set and assessment of our interests to one of exploring the world outside our bodies. Essentially, this is the world in which you must compete, and it is important that you learn the workings of the marketplace regardless of your career aspirations. We will discuss branding, looking for underserved needs, and developing a value proposition in this section. All those terms are fairly well understood by a student of business but can be intimidating or even totally misunderstood by someone who is not trained in business topics.

However, do not despair. Although we will use those terms in the coming chapters, we will go beyond the simple definitions and present the material in a way that can be both understood and embraced, regardless of your professional training. Suffice it to say that your brand is nothing more than how people perceive you. The underserved need is nothing more than an opportunity that does not have a lot of people pursuing it, and a personal value proposition is simply you presenting what you do in a compelling way so that someone would be willing to pay you to do it for them.

Please do not despair or think that these chapters are just for business students. They are for everyone who wants to pursue a viable and exciting career in today's modern work environment. So, on with the development of the processes we need to follow to help us connect more effectively with the external world.

5 Building Your Personal Brand

One process that will help you in your connection with employers and will go a long way in helping you with your self-confidence is to develop a personal brand. The world has changed, and it is important for everyone in the job market to understand the magnitude of these changes. The need for companies to be flexible and to bring people into their companies at a moment's notice has increased significantly. In order to be competitive, companies must be agile and able to respond to changing market conditions quickly and effectively.

As a result, their relationship with employees is constantly changing. They may need your skills for a short time and then no longer need you until another project presents itself. Or they may need you to perform a certain function today and a different one tomorrow. It is highly unlikely that you will continue to work for the same employer, doing the same thing, for an extended time. Even if you do stay with the same company, you will probably work for several different divisions within a company throughout your career. It is crucial that you develop a personal brand that will endure through all the changes and turmoil.

Think about the people you know who are successful. What do they stand for? What do you think of when someone mentions their name? What about Steve Jobs? He is an easy one. Nelson Mandela is another famous person. What do you think of when someone says his name? How about courage, dedication, and commitment? Those are all part of the personal brand that he developed, and it was not easy.

The people who come to mind have clearly developed a personal brand. You know what they stand for and can easily summarize it in your own words. This has happened largely because of their untiring commitment to an idea or concept, and many of them are successful because the idea has something to do with service to humanity

I am not saying that you must give up all your personal possessions and go live in commune. And the idea of trying to be like Steve Jobs or Nelson Mandela is definitely outside the realm of possibilities for many of us. What I am saying is that you must consciously develop your personal brand, and the more you can make it about greatness, the stronger you will feel about it and the more likely you will be able to live consistently within its essence. You want it to be about something that is exciting, even exhilarating, and something you are proud to share with an employer.

WHAT IS A BRAND?

Let's drill down a little further into this concept of branding to give you some insight into how to develop one. The first step is to simply identify what a brand is. According to the dictionary, a brand can either be "a mark made by a hot piece of iron" or "a class of goods identified by name as the product of a single firm or manufacturer." When we talk about a brand, it is more of the second definition than the first, but the concept of permanence, as well as the idea that a brand is not easy to create or duplicate, are all important concepts.

For our purposes, let's think about your brand as simply how you are viewed by the people you engage with in a professional setting. It shows up in how you talk, how you present yourself, how you dress, and the types of work and people that you associate with. Do not be naïve and believe that people are not evaluating you all the time. Your personal brand is constantly being communicated and reinforced to those around you.

You do not need to be paranoid and worry about what they say, but do recognize that how you act and what you say is all part of how your brand is being communicated. This is one of the reasons I recommend you do not post information about yourself on Facebook or other social media that would contradict the brand that you are trying to project. Branding is in line with your professional persona, and employers look at social media sites for information on potential candidates. As you develop your personal brand, be sure you are consistent in every way you communicate. Your brand is how you are perceived by the public, and it must be nurtured, developed, and ultimately, protected.

WHY DO YOU NEED ONE?

Having a brand is actually a tough responsibility, or at least, having the kind of brand you want may be difficult to accomplish. After all, we all have a brand. It is what people think of us when they meet us. The key is that you must manage yours in order to gain the maximum advantage.

Why would I care? Why do I need one? The most direct answer to these questions is, if you are going to think like an entrepreneur, you must be able to present yourself in a positive and valuable manner—and that will involve your brand. It is not a matter of whether you need one. You already have one. People have a perception of you right now. The key is to ask yourself, if your current brand is what you want it to be, how can you continue to build it? And if not, what can you do to change it?

MAKE IT GREAT!

Even though you may not be a business executive or a politician, your personal brand can be rooted in a sense of greatness. Make it worthy of you and your efforts. Allow yourself the opportunity to think about what you can be, and do not be limited by what you have been.

One way of doing this is to take a minute and describe who you would be and what would you do if resources were not an issue. Assume that you have all the money you need and all the available skills and training, and then let yourself go to describe the brand that you would be able to achieve. We are only limited by our own constraints, so take the time to be a little daring. In using the idea of greatness, make your personal brand something that is worthy of you and your efforts. It is more than just being good with Excel or a good problem solver. Make it about who you are and the greatness you can bring into the world.

I know that this sounds like I am one of those motivational speakers who sell a lot of hype without much substance, so please bear with me a little longer. I have had the opportunity to work with many wonderful people throughout my career, and the ones who have had an impact on me and my personal life all have a simple and engaging personal brand. There is no reason everyone cannot have a powerful brand. Think about yours. Identify what it is and nurture it.

If you know some people who will give you honest feedback, ask them what they think your current brand actually is. You do not need to use the word brand but can simply ask them to give you a few key words that describe you. If you work in a company that conducts performance reviews, that can also be a great source of feedback on your personal brand. Take the time to find out what your current brand is and then either continue to develop it or look for ways to change it to be what you want it to be.

PERSONAL MISSION/VALUE/PURPOSE

We all have things that are very important in our lives. Dr. Peter Koestenbaum, in his book *Leadership, The Inner Side of Greatness* talks about 5 major possible themes in our lives. He identifies these as: 1. work, 2. family, 3. self, 4. social responsibility and 5. financial stability. He then goes on to define these more discretely in terms of *vision, reality, ethics and courage*. If you have an interest in doing a deeper dive into these leadership concepts, I recommend that you add his writings to your reading list.

However, for our purposes, you might want to take these 5 areas of focus and think about what they mean to you. In addition, many writers will encourage you to develop a personal vision or values statement to guide you in making the decisions that are consistent with these values. I too would also recommend that you take an approach that enables you to take stock of what is truly important to you and then write it down in some form of a mission or purpose statement. You certainly can consider drawing from Dr. Koestenbaum's model in order to group the areas of your life into a meaningful and tangible context.

Then, when you have it written down, put it someplace where you can refer to it often. You can use it as a reminder of what you should be doing on a daily basis but also to continue to reinforce in you, what you want your brand to be and how you want others to think about you.

PERSONAL BRAND IS "TABLE STAKES"

If you have ever played a game of poker, or even watched someone play, you understand the idea of table stakes. Essentially, it is the idea that when you enter a game, you have to bring something to the table. Whatever you bring are your "table stakes." During the game you cannot bet more than what you have brought to the table.

We are borrowing the term to help focus the concept regarding your personal brand. In essence, your brand reflects your "table stakes." It is what you bring to the table and it is very difficult to change those stakes, or your brand, in the middle of an engagement. You must prepare before you get into the game and know what your brand is and what you are willing to bring to the table.

One other thing to consider is that everyone else is doing the same thing. So never believe that your brand or your "table stakes" will guarantee that you win. It is merely a price of entry. It gets you to the table, and you will then be able to engage fully in the pursuit of your objectives. Your brand can be considered as a necessary, but not sufficient condition, that you need to achieve your goals. However, it is needed, it is important, and it is extremely valuable, so be sure to take the time to focus on the development of it. It will get you into the game so that you can then demonstrate your true value.

KEY ELEMENTS OF
YOUR PERSONAL BRAND

To further define your brand and to better understand the elements, I would like to expand on a concept that was part of a presentation made in 2014 on personal branding at the Washington State Chapter of the Urban and Regional Information Systems Association. At the conference the idea of a personal brand was presented in three domains. They are the Persona, the Promise and the Promotion. I believe that each of these areas are very relevant to our area of focus and so I would like to build on them and apply many of the ideas that we have been developing, and will develop, within that general context.

YOUR PERSONA

If I were to say "Apple computer," what would you think? Do you think of the clean lines, the ease of use, or even the fact that the company focuses on a few great products? By the way, focusing on a few great products is one of the key concepts that Apple is integrating into its advertising campaigns. The company wants you to think of a few great products when you think of Apple, and not a myriad of different products. It is a clear part of its marketing strategy and brand management. You might think about these things as the "heart of the company" and they represent Apple's persona.

What about you? Give some thought to consider what is truly your persona. What is important to you personally? What do people who are close to you think about you? What is core and fundamental and part of what truly makes you who you are? All of these elements add up to represent your persona.

YOUR "SUPER POWERS"

A second element within the context of your brand and its development can be summarized in terms of your personal "Super Powers." I like to use that term to convey the idea that you are unique and that you do bring to the job market unique skills and abilities. It does not matter if you are going into a job that is normally staffed by people with a certain skill set or college degree. You bring your unique perspective and ability to that job. This unique sense of who you can be is very powerful and valuable if you frame it in the context of a "Super Power."

Essentially, this part of your brand is what people at your job, or in your class projects or even if you are involved in volunteer activities, see in you. As a result of your "Super Powers," they will either want to be around you, be indifferent or potentially even want to avoid you. Do not miss the opportunity to think about the unique value that you bring to the current situation, nourish it, reinforce it, remind people of it and help define it in a way that makes you proud and happy to tell people about your super powers.

Now, this might seem a little corny, but it is a concept that marketers are very knowledgeable of and use in many advertising promotions. You can be just a valuable and powerful and inspire those who work around you. There was an effective Coca-Cola TV commercial several years ago in which a football player named Mean Joe Green walks down the tunnel after the game. He looks tired and definitely needs something to pick him up. A young boy appears and gives Green a drink of his Coke. Green thanks the young boy and then, as the boy starts to walk away, tosses him his jersey and thanks him for the Coke. It was a great commercial, and it was clear that Coca-Cola was the providing their "Super Power" to Green and the audience can partake in the "Super Power" of a Coke also.

YOUR PERSONAL STORY

A key part of a brand in our world is the heroic element that reflects your "Super Power" but goes deeper. As Jeff Bezos, the founder of Amazon, once said: "Your brand is what people say about you when you are not in the room." When others think of you, do they think of greatness, service, impact, or other elements that are worthy of your efforts?

The reality is that you are writing your story every day. When you have a cup of coffee with someone, or volunteer to take on an assignment, or offer to help a fellow student, you are writing your brand.

I know that it can be a tall order to always focus on how your brand is being written, but here are <u>four</u> elements of a strong brand, and maybe they can guide you in your daily choices as you craft your personal story.

Brands are **memorable**. If you cannot remember the brand, that company has probably not done a good enough job in developing brand recognition. There is something about an effective brand that makes it memorable. Ask yourself, what do you do to make yourself memorable? What do you want people to think about you and then what are you doing to help them remember you in that light? If you want to be known as a strong problem solver, then you must do things that convey that image to other people.

A second element of a successful brand is that they are **relatable**. People can connect with them. Even if it is for an expensive piece of jewelry or clothing, the brand can convey a sense of exclusiveness with the belief that people will aspire to being able to own that product someday. Now, you do not need to come across as being exclusive or unreachable for people to be able to relate to you, but you do want to give some thought as to how much others can connect with you. Do they feel comfortable approaching you with questions? Are you consciously taking action that would help them think of you as a role model? You simply want to be relatable. You want people to be able to feel some form of connection with you.

The third element is that **people feel good** when they are associated with the brand. They can relate to the brand, but even more important is the ability of the brand to make someone feel good. If you can nail this concept, people will want to be around you. They will feel good when they are connected with you and that will even further help you promote your brand. Pay attention to how people react when you are with them. Are you helping them feel good by being with you? It too is a tall order and can be quite a challenge, but if you want your personal brand to be effective, borrow these ideas from branding literature and apply them in your own life.

The fourth element is that a brand is **persistent and long lasting**. How effective would McDonald's be if they used the Golden Arches and Big Macs to convey their brand this week and then used some other symbol or item from their menu the next week? Now, that is not to say that they cannot change their menu and they certainly do that from time to time, but it is done with a great deal of test marketing and only pursued when they are fairly certain that it will not damage their core brand and will potentially reach a new market or enhance their appeal.

It is the same with an individual brand. You cannot be changing it every week. If you do, your brand will be representative of chaos, and people will not know where you stand on anything. That is why it is so important to take some time to think about what you want your brand to be, and then purposefully manage it on an ongoing basis.

Remember, we all have a brand. You have one right now. Think about it and ask these questions: Is it memorable, is it relatable, do people feel good when the associate with your brand and is it persistent and long lasting?

Use these concepts to help shape your brand and then continue to use them to guide you as you further develop your brand and make tweaks to it along the way. If you want your personal brand to be effective, people must be able not only to remember you but also to relate to you. They need to want to be around you, and they need to know that you will be here tomorrow.

CREATING AND NURTURING YOUR BRAND

How do you go about creating and nurturing your personal brand? Begin by writing it down. Think about the three or four key things that you want people to think of when they come in contact with you. Make your brand great. Make it exciting. Make it something worthy of your lifelong pursuit, and make it difficult to achieve. Nothing worth doing ever comes easy. Your personal branding process will be a work in process, so get started with it, practice communicating it, let it continue to flourish, and be proud of it and what it stands for.

Some ways to communicate your brand involve having a great elevator speech and creating your own personal web page with your message. Also, we will talk more about creating an electronic portfolio, an emerging career-planning tool that can go a long way in articulating your personal brand.

However, remember to be consistent and stay true to your message. If you choose to adjust your brand, do so carefully. If you change your brand on a daily basis, you will create an unintended brand of confusion and inconsistency. Stay faithful to your message. Great companies have built strong brands over years by

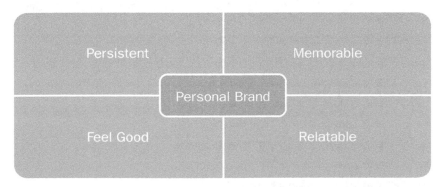

FIGURE 5.1. CHARACTERISTICS OF A STRONG PERSONAL BRAND.

consistently staying on their main message. They may adjust some of the elements, but the main elements persist. Do the same thing. Keep your message consistent and only change it after you have given it some serious consideration.

ADDITIONAL RESOURCES

Here are several websites that can help you in your quest for personal brand development.

Washington State Chapter of the Urban and Regional Information Systems Association Conference—2014 http://www.waurisa.org/conferences/2014_Conference_Index.php

Tom Peters! http://tompeters.com/

"The Brand Called You," Tom Peters, http://www.fastcompany.com/28905/brand-called-you

Branding Pays http://brandingpays.com/

Smarter Networking http://www.smarter-networking.com/main/index.php

Reach Personal Branding http://www.reachpersonalbranding.com/

Training, Coaching and Speaking Services, Pat O'Malley http://arrowleaf.net

PricewaterhouseCoopers(PWC)http://www.pwc.com/us/en/careers/campus/programs-events/personal-brand.html#overview

In addition to these websites, here is a list of 10 skills employers say they seek, in order of importance:

1. Ability to work in a team
2. Ability to make decisions and solve problems
3. Ability to plan, organize and prioritize work
4. Ability to communicate verbally with people inside and outside an organization
5. Ability to obtain and process information
6. Ability to analyze quantitative data
7. Technical knowledge related to the job
8. Proficiency with computer software programs
9. Ability to create and/or edit written reports
10. Ability to sell and influence others

Take a close look at these sites, along with the list of skills, and use them to help inform you in the development of your personal brand. Remember, we all have a brand, and if you do not choose it, it will happen without you controlling it. Your brand is too important to be left to chance. Take advantage of these resources and the other concepts covered in this chapter and develop a personal brand that will truly serve you now, and into the future.

NOW WHAT?

Keeping in mind what we mentioned about greatness and the idea of building a powerful brand, here are some immediate steps you can take to help turn your desired brand into a reality.

1. Start by reviewing your personal career plan and identify some of the following items that you would like to pursue and that can help you further develop your personal brand. Write them down. Make the commitment to do them and then follow up and celebrate after you have completed them.
2. Ask your friends for input on how they see you. Write their answers down. Then think about what your current brand is and what you need to change for your brand to become what you want it to be.
3. Give some thought to who you want to reach and how your brand can help you do so. Identify your goals and priorities, along with your target audiences, and give some thought as to how best to connect with those audiences.
4. Give some preliminary thought to how you are communicating your brand. We will discuss these topics further in chapter 6 but for now, think about how you might pursue some of the following ideas:

    a. Launch your social networking/LinkedIn and blogging.
    b. Get a business card.
    c. Start a web page.
    d. Practice your elevator speech.
    e. Nurture your network.

5. If you have time, write a book, a blog, or some other form of publication. Strive to be known by your brand and consistently look for opportunities to share your brand with others using the written form.

Obviously, this is an extensive list. You do not need to do all of them, but each will add to the strength of your brand. Think about companies whose brands are well known and then commit to the steps that will help yours gain a comparable level of exposure ... at least in your immediate circles.

REFERENCES

Bezos, Jeff *(quoted) How to build your personal brand*, https://www.theguardian.com/careers/build-personal-brand

Koestembaum, Peter *Leadership, The Inner Side of Greatness*, Josey Bass, 1991.

Mapping your Unique Value: A Roadmap to Personal Branding, Washington State Chapter of the Urban and Regional Information Systems Association Conference—2014

Ten skills that employers say they need, Forbes Oct 11, 2013.

6
Articulating Your Personal Value Proposition

WHAT IS A PERSONAL VALUE PROPOSITION?

Now that you have zeroed in on your personal brand, it is time to take it to the next step. In order to do that and to help you answer this question, I am going to challenge you one more time to think like an entrepreneur. If a small business owner wants his or her product or service to be recognized, it has to have value. It does not matter if the owner is a nice person, went to a good school, or lives in a good neighborhood. What matters is the product or service is viewed by the marketplace as having value.

It is the same for you. You have to be able to articulate the value you bring to the market. In order to do so, here are some questions you should ask yourself.

KEY QUESTIONS TO BE ADDRESSED

As you develop your personal value proposition, there are some key questions that must be addressed. None of what we are discussing in this book happen in a positive direction unless there is some consideration given to the external factors that influence the outcome. There are a lot of "influencers" when it comes to your personal value proposition, and it will serve you well to give them due consideration. Paying attention to the following questions will help you ensure that your personal value proposition truly reflects value and will serve as an inducement for someone to want to bring you into their organization.

WHAT IS THE VALUE OF MY CONTRIBUTION?

Think about things you have done in the past that give you a sense of personal pride. What was the outcome associated with that activity, and why was it valuable? Did it delight customers? Did it improve profitability? Did it improve the processes in use in the workplace? The key is to think about any activity in terms of the value it provides.

You have to go beyond simply whether or not you did a good job. For instance, if you finished a project and felt your work done well, is that sufficient? I would argue the answer is no! What was the outcome in terms of someone else who was affected? If you did a great job but it did not have an impact on anyone else or did not contribute to the value of the organization, then it did not have the kind of value we are talking about. You must be able to talk about the outcomes.

When you think about an outcome, take a moment, be critical, get yourself into a mind-set that will challenge you to be the best that you can be and then ask yourself the question "So what?" If you cannot give a definitive answer about positive outcomes, you need to reconsider using this example to demonstrate value.

WHAT EVIDENCE IS THERE OF THE VALUE?

Can I quantify it? Did it improve the organizational metrics in a tangible way? Profitability, customer satisfaction, and process improvement are the big three drivers of value. We often talk about how we improved things, but the more we can back this up with actual results tied to one or more of these three elements, the more impactful our work will be.

This concept can also give you some insight when you consider taking on new initiatives. Ask yourself whether the outcome will be tangible and something you can speak to. It is important to demonstrate this kind of accountability in order to develop your own track record and to build credibility with your leadership team and anyone else who is evaluating your performance.

What are those three or four key attributes that are reflected in these examples of value?

We like to think that we are superhuman, we can do everything, and no one else is quite as skilled as we are at what we do. The reality is that we probably are pretty good at a few things. Take the time to identify what those things are. Write them down. Keep them in mind when you talk about your interests and abilities.

If they represent what you are good at doing and you have tangible examples of demonstrated value associated with these things, you will have a compelling story to tell people. In fact, these three to four key items will be important in many of the sections that follow.

WHO WOULD FIND VALUE IN WHAT I DO?

Even after you have narrowed it down to those few specialties where you are strong and you have tangible examples of the value that you bring to the market, there is still the question of where you will be able to do so.

What kind of employer will need someone with those abilities? What industry will be more supportive of that type of work? And don't forget the government as well as the nonprofit sector when you think about the different environments. The nonprofit sector hires approximately 10 percent of the total workforce in the United States, and government agencies—including federal, state, and local entities—account for more than 10 million jobs projected through 2016. Think about the potential employers who would look at what you do as valuable and want people like you in their organization, and then go after them with a passion.

WHO BENEFITS FROM WHAT I DO, AND HOW DO THEY DO SO?

This is a concept that many entrepreneurs build on when they think about how to enter a market. Part of the idea is to differentiate between a feature and a benefit. The feature of a product is something tangible about it. For instance, a refrigerator may have an external ice dispenser. The benefit is the consumer being able to get ice cubes without opening the refrigerator door.

When you think about who receives the value from your contribution, you might want to think about it in these terms. The feature is what you do, but the benefit is defined in terms of who the final recipient of the value is.

The difference between the features associated with what you do, and the benefits that someone receives from your actions is a very difficult concept for many people to truly appreciate and understand. We work hard. We take pride in what we produce. We are happy with the results and feel that we have been very productive, but if no one benefits from what we have done, we might just as well have stayed home and not even completed the project.

I realize how harsh that may sound. After all, when we try to do our best, shouldn't that be enough? The short answer is yes, but the one that talks about value says that just doing a good job is not enough. In order for something to have value, someone else has to benefit from what you do.

So, the next time you are working on what you feel is an important project either at school or at work, take a moment to reflect on the outcome and think about who will truly benefit from what you have done. The better you get at learning how to focus on the benefit the better prepared you will be for future interviews and other activities when you can talk about your personal value proposition.

Remember, for a business, we are talking about the value realized by the firm through their customers, suppliers, or external stakeholders. There are many ways to bring value to an organization and the better prepared you are to describe how value will be realized as a result of your contribution, the better chance you have to deliver the value.

WHO IS WILLING TO ENDORSE THIS VALUE?

This gets into the whole idea of references and recommendations, which we will discuss later. However, the key here is to identify people who will be able to speak to the specific value you bring to the market. In order for them to do so effectively, they must know your key valuable attributes and how you are able to demonstrate them.

One or two key endorsers will go a long way in marketing your personal value proposition. Take some time to identify and nurture those folks so they can speak clearly about you, your valuable attributes, and how you can bring value to a specific organization.

Take some time to reflect on your value proposition. Begin the process of identifying those three or four key attributes that separate you from the competition. If you are in a business, you have to make many fundamental decisions regarding your product and/or service. Is it going to be unique and hence have a unique value, or is it going to be a commodity and be of equal value with other similar items in the marketplace? If you choose the commodity route, your main option to make a profit is to reduce your expenses to the bare minimum and compete on price alone. However, if your offering has a unique value proposition, you will be able to charge more for your product or service based on the value it brings to the market.

It is the same thing for an individual. Put that entrepreneurial mind-set in place and decide if you want to be a commodity or have a unique value proposition. If you choose the commodity route, then you will have to compete on a global basis with many people who are willing to do your job for a lower price. That is certainly a viable option if you are willing to make that sacrifice, but do not expect that anyone is going to protect your "price" for an extended time. Restrictions on immigration, union contracts, and isolationism can all help stem the tide in the short term, but eventually the pressures of the market will overcome these techniques, and the price for the commodity will stabilize at a global level.

REFERENCES AND RECOMMENDATIONS

You will be asking for references and recommendations at many times in your life. It might be in relation to an application for a scholarship or an award at your university, or it might be for a job or other type of professional opportunity. Regardless of the reason, you will want to be able to ask faculty and/or employers for references from time to time. In fact, when we talk about LinkedIn in chapter 10, getting recommendations is a great way to improve the impact that your online profile will have. When we get there, I will be reminding you that I have seen some wonderful LinkedIn profiles that I know are garnering a lot of interest from recruiters, but I see a lot more that are hastily prepared and are nothing more than a placeholder. If you do choose to jump ahead and start working on your LinkedIn profile, be sure to take time to do it right. It is probably the most critical component of your social media strategy, so invest the required time and be professional.

However, in the meantime, let's take a minute here and talk about recommendations and references in general. When you ask people to be a reference for you, it is a fairly simple task and will not require a lot of effort on their part. Generally, someone will contact them and ask for their input on you and possibly what they feel your strong points are. Just be sure to ask if others are willing to be a reference for you before you give their name to the recruiter. Also, offer to give them a couple bullets about things you would like for them to cover. I am not advocating that people lie for you, but if you are strong at project management but did just OK in accounting and you are asking a professor to give you a reference, he or she might focus on the accounting ability and totally miss the fact you are looking for a project manager opportunity.

The second way you can ask for help is through a recommendation. Realize that it will take a little more effort to write you a recommendation, either on LinkedIn or in a letter, so give your references some substance to use in the recommendation. If you are asking others who know you well for help, they likely will want to help you—but make it easy for them. References and recommendations are used in a myriad of settings, so be sure to do the proper preparation and ask people for the appropriate item, along with offering to provide them a list of topics they can use in the write-up.

BUILDING YOUR PERSONAL VALUE PROPOSITION

If you were going to hire someone to build a deck on your house, you would expect the person to be able to show you pictures of decks he or she had completed in the past. If you were planning to buy a car, you would check the car's maintenance records to see how reliable it is. The list goes on. When you choose to make a purchase, you want some confirmation that what you are buying has a positive value proposition.

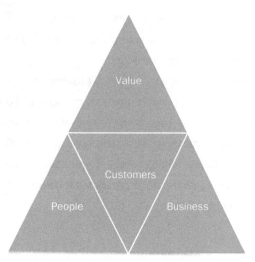

FIGURE 6.1. ELEMENTS THAT A STRONG PERSONAL VALUE PROPOSITION WILL SERVE.

It is the same in the employment scenario. Potential employers will want to know about the value you can bring to their organization. They want to know what you have accomplished, in tangible terms that are valuable to their organization. If you were a small business owner, you would be showing results of your past accomplishments. It is the same thing for you as an individual looking for a career opportunity.

One concept to use to help build and communicate your value proposition is that all firms, regardless of their size or whether they are for-profit or not-for-profit, have three key drivers of success. These three elements are as follows:

1. They need good **people**, and you must be able to talk about how you can help people in the organization be more successful. This might involve good teamwork, project management, or communication skills. Whatever it is that you can bring that will help the people in the organization be more successful is important.

2. They must have **customers**. No matter how good a company thinks its product or service is, it is dead without customers. You too must be able to talk about how you serve customers. What have you done to delight customers in the

past? By being able to talk about customer satisfaction, you reinforce your understanding of its importance and further the employer's positive perception of your personal value proposition.

3. Lastly, any company needs to run like a **business** and have more money coming in than it has going out. It does not matter if it is a for-profit or not-for-profit company. If you have more expenses than revenue, you are out of business. You too can capitalize on this concept and talk about what you have done to improve profitability where you have worked. How have you increased revenue and/or reduced expenses? It does not matter how much, just that you have done so.

PEOPLE

As you think about your value proposition, take these three factors into consideration. The first element involves the operational processes of the firm. Global competition, evolving technology, and new entrants into the field all put pressure on a business to continually improve its processes. As an entrepreneur, you would constantly be challenged to improve operations, and again, it is crucial for you to be aware of these factors in your career planning.

Operational efficiency and helping people be more productive covers project management, communication, team building, leadership, and other factors that involve people in the organization continually improving how they perform tasks. In describing your personal value proposition, you must be able to discuss how you have contributed to an organization's operational efficiency in much the same way you would if it were your own business.

CUSTOMERS

You have all heard the expressions "The customer is king" and "The customer is always right." They are true statements. If you do not have a customer, you are out of business. Think about the times you have served customers. Were they delighted with your service? Did they come back for more? Did they tell others about your work? If you were an entrepreneur, you would live and die by what your customers say about you. It is the same in the career development process. Pay attention to who your customers are. Be sure to nurture them. And if possible, ensure that when you finish dealing with customers, they are happy with the experience.

BUSINESS

Think about the times you have been involved in financial transactions. Did you make good decisions regarding money? Were you able to identify ways to reduce expenses? How about new revenue sources? Were you able to help grow the business by bringing new sources of revenue to your company? You must be able to convey the fact that you treated the financial resources in your experience the same as your own money.

It might have been part of a school project or even a new piece of equipment you purchased. It really does not matter what the project was. What is important is that you convey the sense of accountability and responsibility you assumed as part of your role in dealing with financial resources.

Even if you are waiting tables or working in a gas station, these factors apply to you. They are universal. Anybody in business needs to be responsive to these factors. If you are thinking like an entrepreneur, you will be cognizant of them and constantly aware of the impact you have on them. If you choose to ignore any of these factors, you would fail as an entrepreneur—and you may not be successful in the pursuit of your career development plan.

A personal value proposition is what separates those who have done the work from those who only have the potential. In developing your value proposition, you should do your research, identify the types of roles you want to pursue, and take stock of your experiences and prepare to share them with potential employers.

However, if your value proposition is not as strong as you want it to be, develop a plan to make it stronger. You can do so through purposeful volunteering, unpaid internships, or other ways to build your track record and subsequently your personal value proposition as you launch into the career development process.

The bottom line is you must have a personal value proposition in order to be competitive. Even if you are just starting out in a given career field, you need some experience beforehand. And that experience must focus on customers, profitability, and organizational efficiency. This makes all the difference in the job-search process and will help you be able to clearly articulate the value you can bring to a potential employer.

You build your value proposition one step at a time. You must gain exposure to the field and then engage in activities to help you practice your skills and abilities and ultimately achieve mastery in your area of expertise. It is an ongoing process but one that is critical in order for you to constantly stay ahead of the competition and maintain your edge in today's job market.

SWOT

Any decent strategic business plan will highlight the strengths, weaknesses, opportunities, and threats associated with the business venture. Doing a SWOT analysis is a common process for anyone who is considering launching a new idea and is a powerful tool in helping you develop a better sense of your personal value proposition.

These four cornerstones of any decent strategic plan are also appropriate in a career-acceleration plan. You have to know what you are good at as well as where you are weak. You have to do an assessment of the opportunities that exist as well as the potential threats that might get in your way.

To some degree, this concept will actually run throughout the entire career-planning process. We always need to monitor these four elements because they will change over time. A successful entrepreneur is in touch with them on an ongoing basis, and you too need to be monitoring them.

However, to be a bit more specific, let's take each one and talk a little about how best to track that specific element.

STRENGTHS

Take some time to decide what you are strong at doing. There is a great book you can use to help do this personal inventory: *Now, Discover Your Strengths* by Marcus Buckingham and Donald O. Clifton. Their basic premise is you should understand where you are strong and spend most of your time developing your ability in those areas.

There is a high degree of credibility associated with this idea. We sometimes spend way too much time trying to "fix" areas in which we are not strong. Certainly, if you have a glaring weakness that is getting in the way of you being able to function, you must address it. But other than that, the argument is to focus, and further develop, your strengths.

When you think about it, you will come to realize your strengths exist within you for a good reason. They are there because you enjoy doing that kind of work. You find yourself gravitating to that kind of behavior. Also, there is a definite tendency for you to surround yourself with people who have a similar bent. Your strengths attract others with the same interests, and you continue to build those strengths through practice and interaction with these people.

Listen to what the universe is telling you. The whole idea is not supposed to be difficult. You will find that when you perform in your areas of strengths, things are easier, they tend to make more sense, and you are more at peace with yourself and your surroundings. Take the time to identify where you are strong, and allow yourself to explore and flourish in those areas.

WEAKNESSES

Taking a further page from Buckingham and Clifton, you really do not want to spend a lot of time trying to improve your weaknesses. However, it is critical for you to identify them, especially if they are stopping you from achieving your goals. Think about the things that you do not do well, make you nervous when you have to do them, or do not give you a good sense of accomplishment once they are completed.

This is where it can get a little tricky. There is a common argument about your comfort zone that goes something like this: If you identify those items outside your comfort zone and force yourself to do them, you will feel your comfort zone grow. Maybe public speaking is in this realm. If you hate to give public speeches and you force yourself to do so, you will probably get to the point where it is less painful to give public speeches, and as a result, your personal comfort zone has grown a little.

The key is to listen to what your mind and body are telling you. If making public speeches is opening up a new world for you and you become excited about doing it, then take it and run with it. But if that is not the case, it is perfectly acceptable to consider that skill to be something that you can and will do if necessary, but it will never become one of your strengths.

The bottom line is to continually take inventory of your weaknesses, choosing the ones that you can turn into strengths but accepting that there may be others you only perform when the occasion arises. It will provide you with insight into the kinds of career opportunities you want to explore.

OPPORTUNITIES

This is the area where I have some specific personal experience that is actually quite embarrassing. Several years ago when I was working for an IT company, a salesman made a presentation to me about some new software that was being developed that would plot street maps on my computer. At the time, the personal computer industry had not really taken off, so the computers we used were large IBM mainframe systems, and the monitors were big, clunky, and restricted to the desktop. The particular software he was demonstrating was slow and the output fairly crude.

As I reviewed the demo and the supporting proposal, I wondered why anyone would want to have access to maps on a computer. Everyone had a perfectly functional printed atlas with maps of anywhere they would ever want to go sitting in their desk. Furthermore, the atlas was portable, updated on an annual basis, and easy to use. A map on your computer, which was not portable at this time, did not seem to have much value. So I politely listened to the salesman, took his card, and did not think about it again.

Fast-forward thirty years of more and think about a time when you don't use Google Maps or some other form of GPS technology to help you get where you are going. I am not sure if you can even buy printed atlases in the store anymore.

The point is, I was looking at the opportunity from my current vantage point— mainframe computers, with dumb terminals on my desktop—while others were thinking of computers as being portable and ubiquitous in their environments.

I have come to realize that opportunities are all around us and the key is to be able to see them from a different perspective than we currently possess. One way to expand our perspective is to read business publications and technical magazines. I try to read the *Wall Street Journal* but also keep up with *Fast Company* and *Wired* to stay abreast of current opportunities as they evolve. Also, the more you surround yourself with people who want to push the envelope regarding new ideas, the more you will stay aware of potential opportunities. Hang around with entrepreneurs even if you never want to start your own company.

Again, an entrepreneur is looking for ways he or she can bring a new opportunity to the market. You have to do the same thing and be open to the infinite possibilities that exist in our world.

THREATS

Threats can be both real and imagined. A real threat is when someone from the other side of the world is willing to do what you do for half the price and at a higher quality. An imagined threat is when you *believe* that someone from the other side of the world will soon be willing to do what you do for half the price and at a higher quality.

The point is that it really does not matter if a threat is real or imagined. The real threats may have a more immediate impact, but the imagined threats deserve the same level of urgency and response.

You must constantly think about what you do, what value you bring, and what your unique skills and abilities are, and you must realize there currently is, or soon will be, someone sitting in an office/garage/home getting ready to do the same thing at half the price.

We have talked about this elsewhere in the book, and again, I don't want you to become paranoid. But you do need to think about the factors that threaten your livelihood. If you are running a small business, the threats can be competition but can also be the possibility of one of your key team members being drawn away to work for a competing firm. Or you might lose a key contract with one of your valuable customers.

The same factors actually apply to you as an individual. You may lose a current capability you have. It might be a function of something happening to you personally or to someone in your life who is important to you. Your current employer may be forced to make some tough decisions, and you can wind up getting laid off through no fault of your own.

Suffice it to say, you must constantly be on the alert for potential threats to your career and your prospects for future opportunity. Do not be naïve and believe that once you have an opportunity nailed down, you will always have it. There are always some storm clouds forming in the distance. Be aware of the potential for disruption and put plans in place to ensure the storms have a minimal impact on your life.

FINANCIAL SECURITY

We all want to have some degree of financial security. If you told me you were not worried about making enough money to give you the lifestyle you desire, I would wonder if you were telling me the truth. It is true that many people are not in it for the money. They are committed to providing a service, having an impact in their community, or serving humanity. These folks must have enough money to live, but money is not the prime driver. You may be part of this community, and if you are, my thanks and appreciation go out to you because I know how difficult that can be. However, for many of us, creating wealth and building financial security is important, and if that pertains to you, then you certainly should give voice to that drive.

Regardless of where you fall on this continuum, the reality is you can have it all. You can pursue your passion and pursue your financial security at the same time.

Actually, I believe most successful entrepreneurs are driven by many of the same concepts that we are discussing. Often it is not about the money but rather the pursuit of an idea that is compelling, challenging, and worthy of their efforts.

What I have come to understand is if someone enjoys what they do, they will be exceptionally good at it and will ultimately earn an income consistent with their level of contribution. And don't forget, a lot of the rewards we receive come in the form of nonmonetary benefits. Personally, I know I have the wonderful opportunity to work with college students, and the pleasure of seeing students mature and launch successful careers is extremely satisfying.

Once again, think like an entrepreneur. Put the pure act of making money into the background and, for now, think about how you can pursue a career that will enable and reward you on a consistent and ongoing basis. Believe it or not, the money will come. Decide on your passion, pursue it relentlessly, and continue to draw from concepts like survive, adapt, and flourish that we discussed earlier. Be entrepreneurial. Look for opportunities to pursue that are good in their own right, and the rewards will come.

However, you want to be clear about your expectations and not lose sight of them in the process. When it comes to making money, it is certainly viable to combine it with your "survive, adapt, and flourish" strategy and establish goals in each of the sections for where you want to be from a reward perspective.

Remember, the reward can be both monetary and nonmonetary, so allow for all the possibilities. But do take the time to be as explicit as you can and document your expectations. If you fail to do so, you run the risk of feeling undervalued as you go through the process. Set your goals aggressively, but be realistic. You might even want to borrow a page from traditional goal-setting literature.

And don't forget the bottom line: Think like an entrepreneur. If you have a goal, you will know how you are progressing toward it. If you do not have a goal, you will be busy but will not have a good sense of where you stand relative to the overall approach, and you run the risk of never being satisfied with whatever compensation you are currently experiencing.

LOVE WHAT YOU DO

In addition to making money, I want to mention a few other things that will serve you well in your pursuit of a solid personal value proposition. The first of these is to learn to truly love what you do. When you are talking with someone about a potential opportunity, it will be clear if that opportunity is truly in line with what you love to do. Now, you do not want to be needy, and we will talk more about how to communicate your commitment to a specific opportunity in chapter 11, but for now, simply make the commitment that you are going to do everything you can to love what you do. Believe me, it shows and will covey a strong sense of your personal value proposition every time you get the chance to speak with someone.

I had the opportunity to speak with one of our caterers at a luncheon event on campus, and I asked him if he enjoyed his job. He was very clear in saying how much he loved it and how strong his passion was for the work that he was doing. I know that I felt at that time, that the meal he was preparing was going to be very good, and his overall personal value proposition was very strong. It works! Love what you do, and it will clearly let others know that you are bringing value into their lives.

MANAGE YOUR FINANCES

A second element to ensure that you are able to talk about your personal value proposition is to strive to remove the distractions that might depress you in telling your story. I recently read that over 60% of college students are carrying a debt of $30,000 or more after they graduate. I realize that that number fluctuates but the key is that there is a lot of debt being incurred by students who are in college.

Now, I realize that you may need to be borrowing money to get through school, but it is important to spend some time to truly understand personal financial management and stay on top of your finances. We talked about the Dave Ramsay material in chapter 4, and you might want to go back and take another look at it if you blew past it.

I also realize that we all want to have some degree of financial security. If you told me you were not worried about making enough money to give you the lifestyle you desire, I would wonder if you were telling me the truth. It is true that many people are not in it for the money. They are committed to providing a service, having an impact in their community, or serving humanity. These folks must have enough money to live, but money is not the prime driver. You may be part of this community, and if you are, my thanks and appreciation go out to you because I know how difficult that can be. Just be sure that you pay attention to the finances and it will go a long way to helping you convey a sense of your personal value proposition.

ABUNDANCE VS. SCARCITY

This concept will serve you well throughout your entire life if you can master it. We have all heard the term about the glass being half-full or half-empty and relating it to the idea of being optimistic or pessimistic. A slightly different twist on the concept is to think about it from the perspective of abundance or scarcity.

When you are operating in a mind-set of scarcity, you are fearful of losing things and cling very tightly to them. You are suspicious of anyone who might want to take what you have and you will be very defensive when someone suggests a different approach to solving a problem. When you are operating in this mind-set, your daily efforts are directed at protecting what you have and so your personal value proposition will only reflect what you currently can produce.

An alternative mind-set is one of abundance. Essentially, you are approaching the situation with the perspective that most anything might be possible and that opportunities will present themselves if we look hard enough for them. It is what has given rise to the success that Steve Jobs was able to realize with Apple. If he had been operating from a scarcity mind-set, he would have been trying to protect the domain of mainframe computers and would never have been able to envision the Apple line of computers.

Again, we are not all going to be like Steve Jobs, but we can definitely take a page from his play book. "Think Different" was his mantra. When you see a problem, don't focus on the problem but rather on how a new approach might be able to solve the problem. There are opportunities all around us. What is now proved was once only imagined. When you get into the abundance mind-set, it is much easier for your personal value proposition to flourish and demonstrate how you can truly help someone and bring value into their lives.

ADDITIONAL RESOURCES

Here is a pretty insightful article by the *Harvard Business Review* regarding 4 steps to take to build your personal value proposition https://hbr.org/2011/11/a-value-proposition-for-your-c

In addition to this resource, there are a multitude of resources on the internet to help you with the basic concept of a value proposition. Here are a few but there are many more. Happy hunting!

http://www.slideshare.net/jkonrath/crafting-strong-value-propositions

https://growthandprofit.me/2013/12/10/developing-your-pvp-personal-value-proposition/

https://www.pongoresume.com/articles/53/value-proposition.cfm

http://www.kison.com/whats-your-personal-value-proposition/

NOW WHAT?

You should begin to develop your sense of your own personal value proposition and then continue to refine it. In order to do so, here are some potential ideas:

1. Read up on the idea of a value proposition in the business world so that you have a strong sense of what *value* means and how you might talk to someone about the value you bring to the marketplace.
2. Check out some of the links included in the "Additional Resources" section and explore many of the other resources that are out there for your use.
3. Pull out your personal career plan and commit to one or two specific items, possibly from this list, that will help you get a better handle on your personal value proposition.
4. Participate in a few networking events and ask people what they feel would be most valuable to them in their business ventures.
5. Identify at least three separate concepts that help describe the value you could bring to an employer, and think about how you might describe those items when you are in a networking environment.
6. Review what you have created, tweak it accordingly, and then try again.

You can always continue to tweak your personal value proposition, so don't let that stop you from starting it in the first place. Develop it, pitch it, listen to the responses, adjust it, and then pitch it again. You will become very good at it, and with a little practice you will learn just how valuable it can be.

The bottom line is that if you can learn to bring value to the market, you will always be employable, but if you cannot articulate your personal value, you will always be expendable. It is up to you to decide where you want to be.

REFERENCES

Bolles, Richard N. *What Color Is Your Parachute? A Practical Manual for Job-Hunters and Career-Changers*. New York: Random House, 2013.

Buckingham, Marcus, and Donald O. Clifton. *Now, Discover Your Strengths*. New York: Simon & Schuster, 2001.

Isaacson, Walter, *Steve Jobs*. New York: Simon & Schuster, 2013

7

Identifying Potentially Under-served Needs

S o far, we have been talking about truly understanding yourself, your brand and the value you can bring to a potential
career opportunity. Now we need to finish this off in terms of
what opportunities are out there and how best to qualify them.

If you talk with successful entrepreneurs, a common theme you
will discover is that they looked for an unmet or under-served need in
launching their idea. It is difficult to be in business if you are just one
of many who are chasing an already well-served need. Entrepreneurs
want to go after an under-served need, and you too want to be able
to pursue that kind of opportunity.

Actually, this is one area where entrepreneurs excel but also
enjoy what they do. It is not about trying to get someone to buy what
you are selling. It is all about understanding what potential clients
need and how you can help them solve their problem. It is fun and
may not always work, but it produces results often enough for good
entrepreneurs to continue to find opportunities and bring value to
their prospective clients. In essence, treat a potential employer as
your potential client.

On the other hand, it is the area where most job seekers choose
to take the quick route and jump to the resume or LinkedIn profile
creation without giving due consideration to the importance of

this topic. Don't do that! I realize that this chapter will outline a lot of work that you can potentially do in pursuit of an under-served need, but if you do it with diligence, telling your story and finding a good match is going to be so much more productive. If you skip over this portion, you will still be shooting in the dark and hoping that someone will give you a job. I know it is hard but I also know that it will yield benefits if you are willing to do the work and truly be entrepreneurial in your search.

Any entrepreneur worth his or her salt will begin by telling you the key is to look for the under-served need. If your approach is simply to go out there and look for an opportunity that can be satisfied by more than a million other candidates with the exact same skills and abilities, you are going to have a tough time, and you will not be finding the under-served need. You want to be able to ask the key questions and look for those unique opportunities where something needs to be done and there are a limited number of people who are capable of doing it. It is as simple and as complex as that. Find your niche. Find the opportunity where you can shine.

The immediate response to this suggestion might be something like: "I have a degree in accounting (or marketing, criminal justice, mechanical engineering, etc.), and that is what I want to do. Why do I need to identify an under-served need? I have already developed a skill and knowledge level based on my education and experience. That should be enough! Shouldn't I simply be looking for an opportunity where a company wants to hire someone with my skills and knowledge?"

The basic answer to that question is yes, but it is definitely a qualified yes. You will more than likely be pursuing a career that is consistent with your education and background. But if you begin the approach looking for someone to give you a job based on some form of degree or certification, you are actually giving up control over what can be the most powerful part of this process. If you are able to begin by looking for those unique opportunities where you can apply your skills and knowledge, but also where there is not a preponderance of candidates already pursuing the opportunity, your prospects are obviously going to be much better.

It would be naïve for me to say this is easy. In fact, this is probably the most challenging part of the entire book. There really is not a lot of charted territory here. Things like resumes and cover letters have been extensively dealt with in the literature, but not a lot of work has been done drawing the link between someone looking for a career opportunity and someone out there with an under-served need.

That is why we want to borrow a page from folks who have actually started businesses in response to an under-served need. Since we make the argument that the two processes are similar, you can learn from successful entrepreneurs and apply many of the same concepts in your personal career development plan.

Also, just as a reminder, in his book *What Color Is Your Parachute?*, Richard N. Bolles spends a great deal of time emphasizing that most of the real opportunities result from networking and not from posting your resume on a job board. The same thing happens with entrepreneurs. Their opportunities come from networking and making personal connections, not from posting their services in the want ads.

CAREER MARKET ANALYSIS

In this section, we will take a look at the three main steps that entrepreneurs take when pursuing an under-served need. They must define their market, assess that market, and then determine the best way to enter the market. Given this philosophy, there are some fundamental questions about **what** the opportunities are, **where** they are, and **how** they can be reached. Pursuit of the under-served need for your career-acceleration plan comes down to understanding these three factors and researching opportunities accordingly.

We will take a look at these three steps, how they relate to career opportunities, and how you can learn from prior experiences and better position yourself to take advantage of an under-served need.

DEFINE YOUR MARKET

We want to begin our market analysis by focusing on what is the true, primary market for our services. This is where it is extremely important for you to be reading business publications such as the *Wall Street Journal* as well as local business and professional publications. It is also extremely important for you to be thinking about your personal brand and value proposition as you think about the market(s)

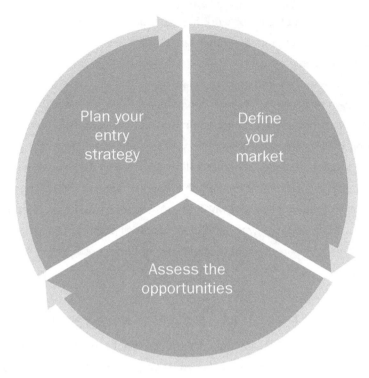

FIGURE 7.1. STRATEGIES TO EMPLOY TO ENTER THE JOB MARKET.

you may want to be pursuing. In addition, you should also be paying attention to seminars and other forms of communication where thought leaders are discussing future prospects of a given environment or even broadcasts and other forms of announcements about your area of interest. Also, you will need to go on several informational interviews. Remember, the best way to gain information about what is going on in an industry or with a firm is to talk to people who are currently working within that specific area. I will continually be reminding you of the value of doing informational interviews in your professional quest. Strive to always have your antenna up and begin to relate what you are seeing with your brand and value proposition. We will be talking about how all three of these elements come together to form your personal "Sweet Spot" in the next chapter, but it is important that your brand and value proposition play a key role in informing your decisions about how to define the market you want to pursue. And in addition to interviews, also take advantage of those chance encounters when you come across someone who can help you better understand the environment. You never know from where the next bit of valuable information will come.

It is critical for you to approach the whole idea of looking at your primary market as a work in progress. You may be able to identify a market that currently exists, but it is equally possible for you to identify an emerging market, one that will be coming online in the near future.

As you read, listen, and ask questions, always be on the lookout for a primary market where you believe you can bring tangible value. Then, as you focus on one or two primary areas of interest, you may need to do some homework and determine the market's needs, current trends, and projected growth levels. You may identify a market that has a high degree of interest for you, but if it has a flat or even declining projected growth curve, you may want to think twice before you go after it.

There are many government websites to help you with this investigation. One of the most valuable and user-friendly sites I use is http://www.bls.gov/ooh, the US government's *Occupational Outlook Handbook*. I recommend you get familiar with it. It will definitely be your friend in this quest. I strongly encourage you to get very familiar with this specific website. It will give you some powerful information regarding the outlook associated with different markets and career fields. However, be sure to view it from the perspective of your brand and value proposition. The temptation might be to pursue opportunities that have some positive growth projections, but if they are too far removed from your brand and value proposition, you might wind up chasing ghosts. Stay focused but do use it to explore potential opportunities that you might not have otherwise considered.

As you qualify your primary market in terms of growth and opportunity, you also want to dive into a better understanding of the different distribution patterns. Do people in that market work in large cities or in rural areas? Do companies purchase their talent through temporary agencies or as direct hires? Are their hiring practices more project related, or do they focus on long-term relationships with their employees?

All these factors are important as you qualify a primary market. You must understand the tendency of employers in order to move away from traditional jobs that provide long-term security to more project-based work that exists until the job is done and the contract terminated. As you review your primary market, you will get a better sense of how the companies in that market engage services. This can actually give you even more of a competitive benefit. For instance, if a primary market is characterized by workers who come on for the project, do the work, and then move to a new opportunity, you have the chance to review that approach and articulate how you can operate in that kind of environment and make flexibility part of your personal value proposition. In essence, the more you know about your primary market and the characteristics of the firms in that market, the better you will be able to position yourself as a valuable candidate for that arena.

Another thing to consider when you look at your primary market is to identify who is your competition. It may be that the companies in this market traditionally hire from Ivy League schools, midsized Midwestern schools, or even schools from a specific state or region. Regardless of the pattern, it is important for you to know who the competition is and how you can package your value proposition to overcome some of the challenges presented by the competition.

One more thing to consider in defining your market is to not fall into the trap of believing that your current job title either limits or propels you to consider a certain job market. I worked with a graduate student who had a lot of project management experience, and it was definitely part of her personal brand and value proposition, but when it came to considering potential job markets, she was not comfortable pursuing some project management–related environments since her former job title did not say she was a project manager. All too often, we get caught up in titles and let them drive some of our decisions. Take the time to get clear about your brand and value proposition and, regardless of what your former titles might have been, make decisions to define your target market in terms of what value you can bring. After all, that is what is most important and will serve you as you continue to qualify potential job markets.

ASSESS YOUR MARKET

Now you have done your homework and identified a primary market, or maybe a couple of different primary markets, where your skills, knowledge, and experience would be well received, and there are ample opportunities for you to explore. Congratulations! You have discovered lots of underserved needs out there waiting for you to respond to them.

The next step is to start zeroing in on the "where" part of the equation. This factor can be related to the city or state where you want to live, or even a more local focus, such as a given neighborhood or region in a city. Also, factors like moving, commuting, or traveling all start to play into this part of the analysis.

Several years ago I was going through a similar process in my life and did not know what was important in my quest. I had done many things and could take advantage of a myriad of opportunities, but I was confused over which of the choices would serve me the best. I wound up taking a little time and simply listed all the potential factors I wanted to consider in evaluating where I should pursue an opportunity. Things like travel, location, rewards and benefits, and even the nature of the people I would be working with or the kind of power or influence I would have over my job or others were all listed. I then went in and prioritized each one. I assigned a 1 if I truly wanted to have it, a 2 if it was OK either way, and a 3 if it was not important.

I am telling you this story because I have come to believe that if you write something down and make it explicit, it will often come into your life. Whether you believe this happens because of a religious conviction or some other cause is not the point. What is important is it happens. Take the time to do it right. Lay out what is important to you. Think about where you want to explore your options and write it down.

I took a good look at my list, reflected on it, and then actually put it aside as I got involved in other activities in my current role. Several years later I came across the list and was happy to see I had made a career decision that resulted in every one of the number 1 characteristics being realized, while some of the number 2 happened, and absolutely none of the number 3 items were present in my current career. I have to admit it was somewhat of an epiphany for me; I came to realize that we can approach the world from a place of abundance, and there are opportunities for all of us out there if we are just open to the possibilities.

Build your own list. Think about the following items as potential characteristics to include in your list. Prioritize them. Put it out there and accept that it is important for you, and when you do, things will start to come into your life that align with these aspirations.

For instance, you might want to consider the following questions:

WHAT IS THE NATURE OF THE WORK?

For instance, does the work involve contact with a lot of clients, internal personnel or even people that are totally outside of the industry? What about the way you contact the people? Is it on the phone, in person, via the internet or through e-mail?

In addition to the ways that you connect with people, what is the actual nature of how you will be producing the work and what is the environment you will be operating in? I once had the opportunity to visit a company in Ann Arbor, Michigan, that was heavily involved in developing and producing computer software for their clients. Now, I had been used to working in an environment where I was in a cubicle and able to focus on my work writing software for our clients. However, there were two things that struck me regarding this firm. The first was that everyone was in an open space, and the tables were movable so that everyone could be moved into, and out of, a given team when it was necessary to form different groups. The second thing that was very interesting was that all the work they did was in pairs. Two people were working simultaneously on a specific piece of software. Now, I thought that I would have had a great deal of difficulty working in an environment like that because I like to focus on the elegance of my programming. The problem with that was that if the code was too elegant, no one else would be able to maintain it.

The key is that you do not want to assume that all work environments are the same. They might be producing a similar product or serve, but the nature of the work can be significantly different. You want to take this into consideration when you are zeroing in on different potential opportunities.

WHAT ARE THE REWARDS AND BENEFITS?

Believe it or not, every company out there does not pay the same nor do they have the same benefit package as everyone else. If it is a well-established company, it might have a well-established benefits package while a newer company might have things like stock options or other equity opportunities for people who are willing to take some risk.

Also, most companies have a compensation strategy where they consciously choose to lead, lag or meet the market. Those that choose to lead are probably in a high growth area and realize that talent is scarce, and they have to be very aggressive in their compensation processes. If they are lagging the market, they believe that the number of potential job incumbents is somewhat saturated, and they do not have to be that competitive to attract new talent. And for those who meet the market, are satisfied that they can attract and reward the talent that they need but do not feel that they have to be overly aggressive.

Companies may not always tell you their philosophy explicitly, but you can gain insight from different salary surveys and then you can ask the company how they administer salary. This is where the whole idea of "pay for performance" comes into play. Listen to what they have to say when you ask questions about their compensation processes. Think about yourself in the company and be sure that you are comfortable with their compensation philosophy.

And lastly, in addition to the structured compensation plans, there are other rewards that may, or may not, be important to you. Will you be in an office or a cubicle? How about vacation time and sick time? Do they allow for you to attend conferences? What about if you choose to write a book or publish a document? Is that encouraged or frowned upon, and who owns what you produce? Again, it all depends on what is important to you but it is worth your time and effort to ask these questions in the determination of which companies and industries you want to pursue.

WHAT ARE THE ENTRY REQUIREMENTS?

It may be a given that they need someone with a college degree. However, that may not be the case. Or, they may need someone with specific experiences or other skills that are not necessarily part of your college program. What about language skills or experience working in a different country? One very real requirement that many companies use is whether or not the candidate did an internship while in college.

The internship question can be tricky because what they are mostly looking for is experience in the areas of what you studied, how you applied it and how you built personal networks in your work. Do not get caught up on the term "internship" because you may be working full-time and cannot take the time to get a formal internship. However, pay attention to this requirement and think about how you might be meeting it through other means. Do not automatically disqualify yourself if you do not have an internship but it is a very common entry requirement that firms have, so you will need to address it.

WHAT IS THE OUTLOOK FOR THE FUTURE?

Pay attention to this question! We all know that everything is subject to change. Think about where the company is going. Try to get a sense for their vision and purpose. Pay attention to how it fits the model of a successful company or is a trend buster? I am not saying that one or the other is bad, but if you are expecting to move into a company that is solid and established and they start talking about changing their processes frequently, you might wind up a little disconcerted.

They key is to think about the future, not just for yourself but for the company and industry that you are evaluating. Make sure that their vision for the future is consistent with yours.

There are other factors that you might want to consider in addition to these. They involve a bit more detail, but you can learn about them by reading their website or even doing research on the company or industry through published sources. (We have included several sources in the addition resources section at the end of this chapter.)

WHAT IS THE STRUCTURE OF THE COMPANY AND HOW IS IT ORGANIZED?

Some companies are organized by product line, some by customer, some by geographic area and some even as a hybrid of a couple of these. That organization structure is often called a matrix organization and you could wind up reporting to two different managers if you are in a matrix structure.

Now, that is not a bad thing, but you might want to give it some consideration as you are doing your industry search. For instance, you might have graduated with a degree in human resources and are looking forward to joining the HR department in your new company. However, when you get there, you realize that you are assigned to the mid western region and are accountable to the team that is supporting operations in that areas of the country. In that role you are reporting to the Vice President of Operations for the Midwestern Region. At the same time, you are also reporting to the Vice President of Human Resources for the company.

Dual types of reporting structures are actually quite common especially since business enterprises have so many complex issues that have to be addressed. Again, you want to go into it with your eyes wide open, so take some time to understand the structure of the company, both from an organization chart perspective but also in relation to its shareholders and other key decision makers.

And don't forget, one of those key decision makers might be the government, and compliance with numerous federal and/or state regulations might also make up a fair amount of the working environment.

WHAT ARE THE DEMOGRAPHICS ASSOCIATED WITH THE WORK?

In addition to considerations about how you might be connecting with your customers, what are the simple demographics associated with the industry? For instance, if you are interested in the auto industry, you will probably be working in large, industrial areas. If it were health care, again it would probably be in larger populated around hospitals or other kinds of health care facilities.

It is probably pretty easy to imagine what the demographics would be associated with a given industry, but the point I want to make is to give it some consideration in the whole process of assessing the different types of industries that you might want to pursue.

WHAT TYPES OF CUSTOMERS WILL YOU BE SERVING?

We talked a little about customers already, but be sure to take some time to think about the kind of customers you want to be working around. For instance, if you are very technical, having customers who also understand technology might be very important. On the other hand, if you want to be able to help people who are not very knowledgeable about a given technology, then that would play into the decision of what customer group would be most inviting for you to pursue.

The other thing to consider is how close you will be with the customer and what will be the reason for the customer to connect with you. If you are working in a held desk environment, it might be possible for you to serve customers frequently but it is entirely possible that they may be upset and difficult to satisfy. However, if you have a role that is focusing on ensuring customer satisfaction, you might have the opportunity to receive positive feedback on a more regular basis.

The customer and your relationship with them is very important and so in your quest, be sure to give ample time to consider the customer that you will be serving and what that relationship is likely to be.

WHAT IS THE PRODUCT OR SERVICE YOUR COMPANY/ INDUSTRY WILL PROVIDE?

It is possible that you may be in a role that is not directly connected to the product or service, but you will want to be part of something that you are proud of and want to share with other people.

One area that some people struggle with is the tobacco industry. You may have nothing to do with the actual production and delivery of the product but you have to be able to work in that industry and not get caught up in the costs or benefits it has for its clients.

WHAT IS THE ACTUAL BUSINESS THAT THE COMPANY IS IN OR THAT THE INDUSTRY SUPPORTS?

A close connection to the product or service is the actual business that the industry is in. Does it promote a lifestyle that you are comfortable with or one that is inconsistent with your personal values? Is it the transportation industry, or the health care industry, or the entertainment industry and what is the actual business model associated with that industry?

It is important for you to understand how a company generates its revenue and what its major expenses are. In order to gain that understanding, you need to know exactly what business they are in and you will also want to know if you are personally aligned with that specific business.

WHERE ARE THE COMPANIES LOCATED AND WHAT ARE THE TYPICAL SIZES?

There are many other factors for you to consider in addition to the ones I highlighted above. You will want to give some thought to the location or size of the organization. Is it predominately in smaller cities or larger one? Is it decentralized and very entrepreneurial or very centralized and bureaucratic? These types of differences can have a big impact on your ultimate satisfaction of working in that industry, so give it some thought and strive to find those that are closely aligned with your personal interests.

DO ANY EXTERNAL PROBLEMS OR CHALLENGES EXIST FOR THE COMPANY/INDUSTRY?

One final thing to consider is the amount pressure from external entities that the company/industry is facing. Are there environmental problems to consider? Are there labor union issues? Are you going to be reading about the company in the newspaper every day?

Now, these do not mean that it is a bad idea to pursue that company/industry. Those problems might be opportunities for you. The key is to just be aware of them and do not get into something that you were not cognizant of. Pay attention and if there are problems, think about how you might be able to help them deal with them.

If you were an entrepreneur evaluating your potential clients, you certainly would be considering these items so it makes complete sense for you to take them into account when you are evaluating which company or industry is most attractive to you and will provide you with the best opportunities.

In addition there are some other types of threats and opportunities that a company or industry might be facing. Things like *emerging technologies*, or *governmental regulations* or *economic changes* or even *industry competitors* all might have an effect on some of the decisions that are being made in a company or industry, and they just might provide you with some further insight into the feasibility of you pursuing opportunities in that space.

All of these challenges can bring either crisis or opportunity. Depending on what you are looking for, you might want to be avoiding crisis or you might be hungry for opportunity. Either way, it is important for you to do a deep dive and better understand the companies and industries that have sparked your interest.

I want to bring one more thing to your assessment that you might not have thought too much about. All companies do not have the same structure when it comes to employing their people. Sometimes an individual is actually hired directly but the company, but often times, they are placed through a third-party firm or even just hired on a temporary basis tied to a specific project that needs to be produced. There might even be a situation where you would sign a contract for a specific period of time and then the contract would be up for renewal.

All of these options have different costs and benefits to both the employer and to you. Being hired as a regular employee may give you more job security and a more lucrative benefits package, but by working with a third-party firm you will have additional support in finding opportunities and the benefits packages might be just as good.

The point is to ask questions and look into the different options available. Maybe a short term, temporary opportunity will be OK for you at the start to get in and demonstrate your ability, but then it would have the downside risk of you not being considered a regular employee.

Just like everything else that we have discussed, it is not that one option is better than the other. It all depends on the situation, the industry, the economic climate and the companies' specific needs. You just want to be aware of the potential opportunities and also try to be open to alternative arrangements that you might not have otherwise considered.

One final thing to consider is the actual competition that you will face. You may have found a perfect company or industry that you want to pursue but if their hiring practices or entry requirements make it difficult for you to get in, you will need to be creative and make yourself even more valuable during the recruiting process.

You also want to be very clear about the company or industry expectations regarding *education level*, their overall *unemployment rates* are, their *compensation philosophy*, the kinds of *experiences* they are looking for and even what kind of *out of the country* opportunities exist.

By now, if you have not already rolled your eyes and said this is way too much, I would be surprised. It is a lot to consider and you are not going to get perfect information in all of these areas. The key is that it is important to consider these factors and don't just decide to pursue a market because you believe that they are hiring.

You want to make an informed decision, and what we are discussing does take much more effort than simply sending your resume out and hoping that your luck will connect you with a great opportunity, but if you do the due diligence, research the companies and industries and strive to make a more informed decision, the probability of you getting involved with a company or industry where you can excel is greatly increased. Be patient, be perseverant and have faith in the outcome. It will serve you well as you decide to take the next step and actually choose to enter the market(s) you have selected.

ENTER YOUR MARKET

Whenever I ask a group of students how they would find out who is hiring, I often get responses such as: check the want ads, ask around, or check with friends. The key is everyone is hiring. Even if you are in the middle of a bankruptcy proceeding, you are hiring. You might just be hiring financial experts who can get you through the bankruptcy procedure, but you are still hiring.

Something to keep in mind is that you should never feel that you have to ask permission to reach out to a firm and inquire about an opportunity. If you have done your homework and determined the primary market and then gone through the process of critically evaluating where you will be able to bring the most value to an organization, companies will want to talk to you. You are valuable. You can contribute to their business, and that will translate into them being interested in pursuing you.

If, on the other hand, you simply send out resumes and ask for someone to give you a chance, your opportunities are much more limited. Do your research. Assess how you can bring value, and then get in front of potential employers with that value proposition. We will discuss reaching employers in the next section, but always be confident that if you are prepared, you will be successful and employers will be eager to have you join their firm.

REACHING POTENTIAL EMPLOYERS

You have done your homework and identified a primary market or two and have done extensive preparation in terms of where you want to pursue your opportunities. Now comes the fun part. You are now ready to actually start making connections with potential employers.

As I have done elsewhere in this book, I recommend that you consider picking up a copy, or at least reviewing the high-level process, that Steve Dalton has laid out in *The 2-Hour Job Search*. In this book he has laid out an extensive process to use in identifying and contacting potential employers. It would be a good addition to your library, and it would be foolhardy of me to try to duplicate everything that he has covered in this book. Suffice it to say that it is a great way to identify, prioritize, contact, track, and nurture potential employers.

If, on the other hand, you want to choose a somewhat simpler route, follow the processes I cover in this section. These will get you going in the employer identification process.

As you prepare to reach potential employers, you must think like an entrepreneur would think. A universal concept with entrepreneurs is that when they approach a client, they must have the ability to talk about the value their product and/or service has for that specific client.

It is your responsibility to be able to identify and talk about the value you bring to the market, and it has to be in tangible terms that have meaning to the employer. Anybody who is making a hiring decision has got to consider the costs and benefits associated with the decision. If you can get into a dialog about the tangible value you bring, you will go a long way in distancing yourself from the competition and showing your value to the employer.

For instance, if you are looking for an entry-level position, you might want to consider applying to work in an internship-type of role. Interns usually work four to eight months or longer as temporary employees and then are often converted to full-time employees after the initial period. There is ample evidence that hiring an intern makes good business sense and has true value to the employer as a recruiting tactic. You can use this to support your case as you present yourself and offer the suggestion to work as an intern for an initial period.

Another option that employers often use is to hire employees from a temporary placement firm such as Manpower or Kelly Services. There are a several reasons for this, but the two most prevalent ones are the placement firm does the sourcing and presents only qualified candidates to the hiring company, and the candidate is actually hired and paid by the placement firm. As a result of this arrangement, when the hiring firm no longer has a need, it can simply terminate the employment agreement, which is usually part of the contractual arrangement with the placement firm.

Here is another opportunity for you to think like an entrepreneur. The first is to present yourself as though you are just as vetted and qualified as the other candidates who are presented by a placement firm. You can do so by clearly articulating the hiring company's needs and showing how you fit those needs. These needs might even go beyond the job description, so think of yourself as providing a service to the employer as though you were a placement firm, except you are the one being placed. Also, consider presenting yourself as a contract employee, which is essentially what the company would experience if it was working with a placement firm. This is a common approach, especially if the company is not ready to make a long-term commitment with a hiring decision. If you choose this path, you will need to set up your own tax payment processes, since the employer will not withhold income tax. You will also need to plan for the absence of benefits from the employer. But it is certainly a viable approach, and one you should give due consideration.

The key is to think like an entrepreneur. What are employers looking for in terms of value regarding their decision to hire a new employee? You have to get past the idea of what is good for you. It has to be couched in terms of what is good for employers. Once you have satisfied employers' questions and they know you are looking out for their good, they will be able to start thinking about what is good for you.

Part of what I am saying is that you do not want to go to an employer and tell him or her why the job is good for you. You do not want to say it will give you the chance to travel, enhance your knowledge in certain areas, pursue a graduate degree, or any of the multitude of reasons why the employer is attractive to you. Think about their problems. Do your homework and learn what they have to deal with, and then present yourself in a way to addresses those problems.

SKIP THE OBJECTIVE STATEMENT IN YOUR RESUME

This is one of the reasons why many authors recommend you do not include an objective statement in your resume: objectives are often written from the perspective of the candidate and what the candidate wants to receive from the opportunity. When you lead with "what's in it for me" instead of "what's in it for them," you start off on the wrong foot.

If you are still convinced that you must include an objective statement, be sure it addresses how you will bring value to the company, and not how the company will bring value to you.

There are actually many different types of employment arrangements you can consider when you present yourself to an employer. Beyond the structure of the actual employment agreement, you can also think about whether you want to present yourself as a new approach to an existing problem or as a similar approach that has been used in the past. What I mean by this is if you were an entrepreneur and were presenting an idea to a potential client, you would position it as either a new and innovative approach or a tried and true approach with possibly a more valuable twist. Think about how each of these would be perceived by the employer, and choose which approach would present you in the most favorable light.

Let's drill down a little more into this concept. Say you are reaching out to an employer and want to present yourself as a new way to address his or her need. Part of that newness could be in the form of the suggested employment arrangement. Maybe you want to offer to be an intern, an independent employee, or some other creative idea about the actual arrangement with the employer. Other types of temporary employment, contingent employment, full- or part-time arrangements, or even working from home are all different ways that you can be creative. It is also entirely possible your potential employer will appreciate your creativity.

Taking this concept a bit further, you might present yourself in a role that is different than expected. Say an employer is looking to hire a web page designer and pay a salary. You could present yourself in terms of how productive you would be and structure the relationship to compensate you based on web pages designed or even some other metric involving desired outcomes, rather than a salary.

There are a myriad of different ways you could structure the relationship, but a high-level way to think about it would be for you to present your contribution as either a totally new way to approach the problem or as a traditional way to approach it, with a valuable twist. Either way, do your homework and be prepared to talk about things like what are the pros and cons or risks and rewards associated with the company pursuing a different hiring arrangement. Will it help them with their competition, or reduce their development expenses. Bottom line, will it yield a positive financial return to their bottom line?

Again, get out of the mind-set of just getting hired to do a job. Get into the mind-set of solving problems and helping the potential company gain a positive financial return from doing business with you. If you do this well, you will be thinking and acting like an entrepreneur and will be better positioned to articulate the true value you bring to the potential employer.

Other things to consider in your creative approach to contacting employers are asking to do some job shadowing and offering to do some temporary volunteer work. These might not work for all employers, but the idea you want to convey is that you are willing to do what it takes to learn and are putting their needs in front of yours. This last point is so extremely important that I want to emphasize it one more time. I have had the opportunity to speak with many recruiters, and the more the candidates are able to talk about the firm and the value they bring to the firm, the better the outcome. It has to be about the employer and not about you, especially in the early stages of the recruitment process.

As far as the actual mechanics of contacting employers, do not feel you must wait for an invitation. Reach out, make connections, ask for informational interviews, network, get a business card, and keep track of who you meet, follow up, and have an elevator pitch ready when you do meet potential employers. We will cover the whole process of networking in a couple other sections of this book because it is so important. However, if you have taken the time to identify your primary market, done your due diligence research regarding the different ways you can pursue that market, and have developed an entrepreneurial mind-set and approach to lead with the value you bring, you will be successful. Take the time to work through these suggestions. This is the way an entrepreneur builds his or her business, and it can be the way you build your career-acceleration plan.

CURRENT KEY RESOURCES
IN YOUR FIELD OF INTEREST

There is some compelling research out there about jobs and what their placement rates are for different types of application processes. Richard N. Bolles covers it extensively in his book *What Color Is Your Parachute?* Essentially, all the research says that most jobs get filled through networking of one form or another, and not by sending your resume to a job board.

It does not hurt to post your resume, but you want to spend 5 percent to 10 percent of your time posting your resume and 90 percent to 95 percent of your time working your relationships. You can believe that entrepreneurs are constantly looking for relationships with people who find their products valuable.

Knowing, or at least believing that one knows, what the customer wants makes all the difference in an entrepreneur's strategy for product and/or service development. It is the same for the job seeker.

You know relationships are important. But how do you get started building them? Here are some easy and direct initiatives for you to pursue.

CONFERENCES

Attending conferences and networking events is a great way to expand your personal network. Also, if you do not have any yet, get some business cards. Even If you are still a student, you can have a business card with your personal contact information on it. You can get the card stock from your local office supply store and then use one of the popular software tools to create a professional-looking business card to share at these events.

One technique I have seen students use is to create a personal web page with a QR code, which they include along with the URL on a business card. You can do the same thing. That way, if people want to learn more about you after you meet with them, they will be able to look you up on the internet.

As you go through the process of providing access to further information about you, be absolutely certain your presence on LinkedIn, Facebook, or any other social media site is 100 percent professional. You can be sure a successful entrepreneur will not have questionable material about themselves, or their company, on a social media site. The same goes for you. You must maintain a completely professional presence on your different sites.

It is certainly acceptable to be sociable and convey that you have interests, but use the acid test and ask yourself if you would want to do business with someone who has a questionable post. Err on the side of being conservative.

NETWORKING

So you have decided to do some serious networking. You have your business cards ready and have checked the local chamber of commerce, professional organizations, and/or websites for events in your area of interest. You have registered for an upcoming event and are going this evening. However, you are a little nervous, so you invite some of your friends to go with you. Sound familiar?

Bringing your friends along to an event is completely normal, and many people do something similar when they are going to an activity and are not completely comfortable with the environment. However, it can lead to a problem! When we go with friends, we tend to hang out with our friends. They represent our comfort zone, so we tend stay close to them. In fact, that feeling of comfort actually reinforces the behavior of sticking together, because it is easy for you to get into the people-watching mode and talk about what you are seeing among yourselves instead of venturing out and meeting new people.

If you go with friends, be sure you separate at the door. You might even want to discuss it a little before the event so you are all on the same page. I used to work with a woman who would literally break off our conversation as soon as we arrived at the event, and I would not see her again until it was essentially over. You can talk with your friends at any time. Take advantage of who is at the conference and make some new acquaintances.

Once you have broken away from your comfort zone, you will want to get the conversation going with someone who is a complete stranger. If you met someone on the street, you would not do this, but you are at a networking event, and everyone there wants to network.

To break the ice, you can simply introduce yourself to people and then ask them what they do. People love to talk about themselves. This way, you do not need to volunteer any information about yourself until they ask. And once they have asked, you have license to talk about who you are and what you do.

Most people will eventually ask you to tell them about yourself. This is where the idea of an elevator speech kicks in. Go back to the three or four key attributes we discussed earlier. Your elevator speech will be built on those key elements. We will discuss this concept more fully elsewhere in the book, but suffice it to know you will need to have practiced a tight elevator speech in order to be confident and impressive in any networking type of event.

Lastly, be on the lookout for people who are in your industry. They might be a great resource to ask for an informational interview at a later date or maybe just a resource to ask a question or two over the phone. The key is to give them one of your cards, take one of theirs, and then send a follow-up e-mail afterward. And lastly, don't forget to organize your contacts into some form of calendaring system so that you can follow up with them in the future in an organized and productive manner.

USING THE INTERNET

And don't forget about the power of using the Internet to supplement your networking strategies. You can follow up on connections you make at conferences, seek out new people based on the networks of the people you meet, and even introduce yourself to new groups when you discover them. The power of the internet is strong, but you want to be sure you use that power to support a deliberate strategy. Use it as a tool, just like everything else we cover in this book, to promote your brand and make valuable connections.

ADDITIONAL RESOURCES

In addition to the resources we included in chapter 3, here are some further resources for you to pursue.

Occupational Outlook Handbook

Bureau of Labor Statistics, State Occupational Employment and Wage Estimates, https://www.bls.gov/oes/current/oessrcst.htm

To become aware of new industries and the jobs they create, read magazines that cover trends, especially in entrepreneurship. Suggested titles are listed below. Find them in print at your local library. The magazine websites offer some free content.

- *Bloomberg BusinessWeek*

- *Entrepreneur Magazine*
- *Fast Company*
- *Forbes*
- *Fortune*
- *Futurist*
- *Inc.*
- *Wired*

The most obvious place to begin research on a company is its website.

If it is a public company, traded on a U.S. stock exchange, you can also go to www.sec.gov for annual and quarterly financials. The reports present an overview of the company's hits and misses and future strategies for growth.

For a third-party viewpoint on **public companies**, try these internet sites which are free, or offer at least some useful, free content among the fee-based content:

- **Hoover's**—Company location; Fortune ranking; top competitors, industry, company profile, year founded, and annual revenue.
- **Yahoo! Finance**—Mainly covers public companies; company description; some news and financials.
- **CNN Money**—Company financials and press releases along with competitor data

In addition to this content, if you are a student within the University of Michigan system, here are some additional resources you can access through the Mardigian Library:
- **Going Global**—contains country career guides, USA City career guides, job postings and internships, H1B Visa employers, key employer directory
- **Occupational Outlook Handbook**—For hundreds of different types of jobs, discover the training and education needed, earnings, expected job prospects, what workers on the job do, and working conditions.
- **USA Career Guides**—Covers career and employment opportunities in the largest cities in North America. Includes business and networking groups, job search resources, and cost of living data.

The magazines below are available through Mardigian Library databases:

- *Entrepreneur Magazine*
- *Fast Company*
- *Forbes*
- *Fortune*
- *Futurist*
- *Inc.*
- *Wired*

Use the following databases and limit your search to a specific journal, if you wish:

- ABI/INFORM
- Business Abstracts with Full Text
- Factiva
- ProQuest Research Library
- Omnifile Full Text Select

Besides the company website and www.sec.gov, use these Mardigian Library databases to gain an overview of an employer you would like to pursue:

- Avention
- Mergent Intellect
- MarketLine Advantage
- Business Insights: Global

To find news on both private and public companies, use databases that include journal and newspaper articles as well as newswire stories. Here are some good starting points:

- ABI/INFORM
- Business Collection

- Business Abstracts with Full Text
- Expanded Academic ASAP
- Factiva
- General One File
- Infotrac Newstand

NOW WHAT?

Where do you begin? It has to be a bit overwhelming but we have all heard the famous quotation "A journey of a thousand miles begins with the first step" by Lao Tzu. This is your chance to take the first step and begin your journey.

Some potential first steps include the following:

Start with your career plan. Make some specific commitments to help investigate potential companies and industries, follow through on your commitments and celebrate your accomplishments.

Organize your approach in terms of:

1. Seeking out Informational interviews
2. Participating in networking events
3. Trolling the internet for opportunities—review companies' web pages who are in your target area and look for ways to help them serve their purpose based on the value that you can bring to the organization. Then, either through informational interviews and/or networking opportunities, find ways to get in front of decision makers and be prepared to talk about the value you can bring to their specific needs.
4. Commit to attending a specific number of networking events in the coming weeks and months.
5. Identify specific goals before the events and frame them in terms of how you can help someone else.
6. Commit to looking for at least one potential opportunity each day in your daily activities and summarize them on a biweekly basis in your journal.
7. Commit to reading professional business publications such as the *Wall Street Journal* and identify at least one potential opportunity from what you read.

There are opportunities all around us, but we have to start looking before they become obvious. Make the commitment to start looking and follow it with definitive commitments so that you can see your progress from week to week. Your thousand-mile journey has just begun, but if you stick with it, you will soon see the progress you are making and will want to continue the quest.

REFERENCES

US Department of Labor, Bureau of Labor Statistics. *Occupational Outlook Handbook*. http://www.bls.gov/ooh.

Lao Tzu—Brainy Quotes—http://www.brainyquote.com/quotes/quotes/l/laotzu 137141.html

8

Developing your "Sweet Spot"

WHAT IS THE "SWEET SPOT"?

How does all this come together in a way that serves you but also can help you be much more attractive to a potential employer? The answer to that question lies in finding your personal "sweet spot."

The sweet spot is where your personal brand, the underserved need, and your personal value proposition come together. As highlighted in the following graphic, the focus is to find where those three elements come together for you on a personal basis.

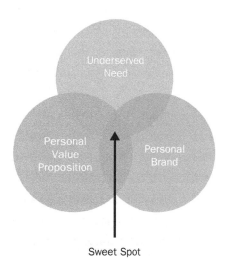

Sweet Spot

FIGURE 8.1. BRINGING THE ELEMENTS TOGETHER TO DEVELOP YOUR SWEET SPOT.

An example of your sweet spot might go something like this. You feel that part of your personal brand is that you are very good at attention to detail and project management. Whenever someone thinks about you, the idea of a master project manager comes to mind.

You have been doing a lot of networking and have met a manager who is struggling with ensuring that everyone on his team knows their responsibilities and that he knows if things are getting behind.

Your personal value proposition is that you are able to demonstrate to managers the value of good project management techniques, especially in response to some pressing customer-related issues.

Here is how the magic of the sweet spot comes into play. You look at the situation that has been presented to you and are able to clearly state that you can put a process in place that will help the manager communicate better with his customer and will have a much better idea of where the project stands. You respond to an underserved need. You play on your personal brand and focus your value proposition to that specific manager, with that specific need that can be satisfied by your specific skills and abilities. If you can learn to manage your "sweet spot" well, you will never have to worry about who will hire you.

Whenever I discuss this concept with business leaders, they all resonate with the idea and confirm that if someone can present their "sweet spot" in a compelling manner, they will be successful. I encourage you to focus on developing your personal sweet spot for every situation that you confront, if it is something that builds on your abilities, and you will be able to clearly show the value. You will not be disappointed.

The idea of the sweet spot is critical to everything we have been discussing. By being able to identify it in response to a real need that capitalizes on your personal brand is the difference maker. It is what will enable you to consistently pursue a viable and exciting career. It is what keeps entrepreneurs in business, and it will keep you engaged in a productive and rewarding career.

So let's do a deeper diver into ways to create your sweet spot, things that might get in the way and some general characteristics that will help you keep it alive and relevant.

ELEMENTS

Let's begin our deeper dive into the "sweet spot" development by doing a quick summary of the elements and pay special attention to how they might come together.

All three of these elements can exist by themselves, in combination with just one other or totally integrated into the "sweet spot." If you recall, the **brand** is all about you and what you want the world to know about it. It can be summarized in terms of your <u>persona</u>, your <u>super power or promise</u> and your <u>promotion</u>.

The **personal value proposition** is how you can translate what you do and what you want people to know about you into a real, tangible statement of the value that you can bring to the job market in general.

And the third element, the **underserved need** is that opportunity that is out there that will provide someone with the opportunity to demonstrate their ability and make a contribution to the appropriate organization, in exchange for some kind of financial or personal reward.

The idea of the sweet spot is critical to everything we have been discussing. By being able to identify it in response to a real need that capitalizes on your personal brand is the difference maker. It is what will enable you to consistently pursue a viable and exciting career. It is what keeps entrepreneurs in business, and it will keep you engaged in a productive and rewarding career.

BRAND AND PERSONAL VALUE PROPOSITION

I want to be very explicit and describe how bringing these two elements together initially, will go a long way in helping you identify viable underserved opportunities that can truly be served by the development of your "sweet spot." You can purposefully bring these two elements together when you have done a good job developing your brand and have thought about how you can bring that brand into the job market in an effective way. You have not yet identified the underserved need but when you have achieved this condition, you are in prime shape to focus on potential opportunities.

A couple of possible examples of this might be something along these lines. An individual has determined that they are very good at attention to detail. They want the members of their teams to rely on them to edit the projects and confirm that the data is accurate in any analysis that has been run. That would represent their personal brand. Furthermore, they know from listening to their professors and reading trade literature that market research has value in the job market, and they are in the process of developing their personal value proposition that will focus on market research opportunities.

Another possible situation might be that an individual is very outgoing, loves to connect with people and wants everyone to know that they are very easy to approach; i.e. their personal brand. They also are able to find opportunities for their student organization to raise funds and have taken a leadership role in the realm of fund development; i.e. their personal value proposition.

This is a very desirable situation to be in and is actually the best place to start in the implementation of an opportunity development strategy.

MAKING THE CONNECTION TO THE UNDERSERVED NEED

So now you have the opportunity to find the underserved need that will connect with the other two elements. In fact, it might be very helpful to think about the creation of the "sweet spot" in two phases. The first is in the formation of the intersection between the personal brand and the personal value proposition. Once you have done that, it is much easier to then look for viable opportunities that are congruent with the intersection of those two elements.

As you become more proficient in the development of this idea, it is possible that you will be able to pursue all three at the same time, but for now, I recommend that you think of it in more of a sequential manner. One way to visualize it is to think of that third "bubble" in our earlier graphic as actually a "floating bubble" and that there are also many bubbles out there. I have tried to capture this concept in the following graphic. Essentially, it is your challenge and opportunity to find the "floating bubbles" that most closely align with your brand and value proposition and then decide which one is going to be the best fit for your brand and value proposition.

If you approach this idea from more of a sequential process, you will be much better prepared to pass on those "bubbles" that appear to be potential opportunities but are not truly part of your personal "sweet spot."

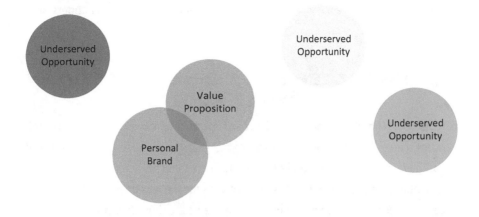

FIGURE 8.2. VALUE PROPOSITION BUBBLES

I have come to believe that this is one of the more difficult things a job seeker needs to master in the pursuit of a good opportunity and that is to avoid being lured by "floating bubbles." They may have gone through the process of identifying their personal brand and value proposition, but when they uncover a potential job that has a salary and a nice benefit package and maybe is at a location where they would like to work, the brand and value proposition get set aside, and the individual winds up applying for the job.

My caution to you is that you do not get lured into taking a position just because it is available. You owe it to yourself to give voice to your brand and personal value proposition. Be critical. Strive to find the underserved need that will truly benefit from what you want to be about and what value you can bring to it.

I fully realize how hard this is, and I also know that there will be times when you opt to take the most expeditions route based on your personal priorities and possibly those from others who are in your influence circle. All I can say is that by this time in the process, if you have truly done your due diligence and developed a strong sense of what your "sweet spot" can be, that you do everything you can to find the right connection.

It is also a work is process and will continue to evolve, but strive to be true to your own personal goals and objectives. The following elements of a powerful "sweet spot" might even give you some further encouragement and understanding in this realm.

CHARACTERISTICS OF A POWERFUL "SWEET SPOT"

Essentially, the idea is that your sweet spot should be compelling, valuable, relevant, current, and expansive. I fully realize that this is not an easy task, but if you have done your work and developed it in a thoughtful and purposeful way, it is attainable and serve you in a positive way for the rest of your life. Make the commitment to develop and continually revise it, use these five characteristics to continue to adjust it and if you can learn to do that, you will never have to worry about who will hire you. Practice developing your personal "sweet spot" for every situation that builds on your abilities, and you will be able to clearly show the value.

COMPELLING

Think about this word a little and reflect on those things that you find to be compelling in your life. Do compelling items cause you to pay closer attention to what is happening? Do they cause you to care more about the outcome? Do they pique your interest?

You want your "sweet spot" to be able to command the same kind of reaction when you present it to a potential employer. If the reaction is not compelling, the employer may be less inclined to follow up with you for that key opportunity. Furthermore, you may be equally qualified for a given position along with several other candidates, but if your "sweet spot" is not compelling, it will not contribute to the understanding of what makes you different from the completion. Think about it, and put yourself in the employers' shoes and ask yourself if your "sweet spot" is truly compelling. Those that are will definitely get more attention from potential employers

VALUABLE

This is the theme that we are constantly reinforcing throughout the entire book. Are you valuable? One way to think about this is from a purely economic model.

Will your "sweet spot" result in a given company getting more in return than what they have to spend for your services? Now, I know that it is almost impossible to put this equation into actual financial terms, but it is still important for an employer to have a sense that the benefit/cost ratio of hiring you is positive.

Take a little time and be critical. Think about what your "sweet spot" will bring and what is the cost associated with a company choosing to hire you. It always has to be in the positive number, and while it can be both objective and subjective, it still has to be perceived as being positive. Again, put yourself in the shoes of a potential employer and critically assess if your benefit/cost ratio is going to be positive. Your competitors will be able to do so, and your challenge will be to do it even better than they can.

RELEVANT

This is where a lot of job seekers can get off-track. They may be very confident in their personal brand and value proposition, but can also fall into the trap of being a little arrogant or naïve in assuming that a given employer will be able to see the relevance of what they can provide.

You actually need to have a little humility with this characteristic. You may be very confident in what you can do, but if it is not relevant in today's job market, it will not serve you well in your quest. This is where you get into the mode. If you treat it from this type of sequential approach you will be much better prepared to pass on potential opportunities that exist but are not truly part of your personal "sweet spot."

CURRENT

Another area that will make you want to keep your "sweet spot" in sync with what is currently needed. I am reminded of my prior career and the fact that my "sweet spot" was largely a function of the fact that I was willing to go anywhere and do most anything that the company needed me to do. I had built that "sweet spot" when the company was young and growing, and they needed people who were flexible and adaptive.

Fast-forward 20 years, and the company had grown so much and had become so well developed, that they did not need people who were willing to go anywhere and do anything. Those elements were still part of my brand and the value proposition I felt I would bring to a company, but they were no longer current.

Needs change. Technology is constantly driving change in organizations. New products and services are constantly changing a company's market conditions, and so the "sweet spots" of the people employed by the company need to constantly remain current. Pay attention to this element both in your initial job quest but also throughout your professional career. If your "sweet spot" does not remain current, you will quickly become irrelevant and replaceable. Take this concept into mind also as you develop and articulate your personal "sweet spot."

And if you want to get a further idea of how jobs are changing, take a look at the following website that lays out 10 hot job titles that did not exist 10 years ago: http://theundercoverrecruiter.com/top-job-titles-didnt-exist-5-years-ago/

EXPANSIVE

This concept is a close cousin to the prior one. Your "sweet spot" must be current, but it also must be able to adapt with the changes that can occur. If it is too limiting, it might serve you today, but it can quickly become outdated. Think about DVD rentals. These companies got locked into the belief that people would want to rent movies from a store on an ongoing basis, and they did not allow for the idea of video being streamed over the internet.

When you think about your "sweet spot," allow room for growth. Pay attention to what is happening in your target industry from the perspective of technology or competition or just plain changes in consumer tastes. These can all affect the value of your "sweet spot," but with a little planning you can positon yourself in such a way that your "sweet spot" can expand to keep up with these changes.

However, if you still need proof regarding how much change is going on in the job market, take a look at the following website: http://theundercoverrecruiter.com/top-job-titles-didnt-exist-5-years-ago/

The only thing that is constant is change, and the only thing you can count on regarding change is that it probably will be speeding up in how fast it happens.

You have to allow for that and keep expanding your personal "sweet spot" just to stay relevant.

'TIS THE SEASON FOR CAREER FAIRS

We have one more thing to consider before we wrap up this chapter. Regardless of whether or not you are currently in school or have graduated and are looking for opportunities, the idea of a career fair might be very inviting. After all, the chance to get a lot of potential employers in a room is like going to a candy store and having your pick of all of the sweet options at your disposal. And the opportunity to have unlimited access to a potpourri of opportunities can totally through you off your game plan.

So, you are reading the paper or you see that there is a career fair coming up that you want to attend. You dig out your resume, hurry down to the fair between classes, try to talk to as many people as possible and don't forget to ask them what they do! Sound like good advice? I hope not because that may be how a lot of students do it, but it is totally wrong. **Don't do any of those things!**

You want to **prepare for the career fair**. Be sure to dress professionally. Work on your personal brand and your value proposition. Know what it is and how you can talk about it when you are meeting with a potential employer. Career fairs can truly be wonderful sources of opportunity if you take the time to prepare.

Perform your "due diligence" i.e. do some research. Given that you have a sense of your brand and value proposition, use this time to sort through the "floating bubbles" and find some that you feel are a good fit and will give you the chance to truly develop your "sweet spot."

Again, this one of the prime opportunities for you to lose your way and get sucked into the lure of who is hiring. After all, the room will be full of the companies that are there are hiring. You get the feeling that they all might be a possible match for you. You do not want to miss any opportunities. You want to be open and wait for the right opportunity to present itself. These are the things that go through our minds. However, I hope that you have a sense of how that might be counter productive to your empowered search. Take advantage of the fact that there are many companies present, but stick to your convictions and only go after those "bubbles" that might be a good match for your personal "sweet spot."

A couple more suggestions regarding career fairs. When you get there, you may be standing in line waiting to talk to a recruiter. Listen to what the student in front of you is asking and what the recruiter is asking of them. This information may give you even further insight into how your brand and value proposition may or may not be a match for them. Remember, it is work in process and will continue to evolve but if you strive to find the key "sweet spots" for your career, you are going to be more successful in both the short and long term.

And lastly, you will have the opportunity to make a **first impression,** so it is extremely important not to squander this opportunity. So take your time, do your research, be clear on how your brand and value proposition can connect with what they need, present a positive image, ensure that you can see how you can bring value to the company and enjoy the experience. You got this!

ADDITIONAL RESOURCES

I am including these resources more from the perspective of helping you find potential "floating bubbles" that you might want to explore. Remember, just because you find an opportunity posted does not mean that it is a good match for your personal "sweet spot." However, this list can give you some great insight into the types of opportunities that are "floating" around out there and that you might want to consider going after.

https://www.monster.com/
https://www.glassdoor.com/index.htm
http://www.careerbuilder.com/
https://www.ziprecruiter.com/
https://www.indeed.com/

Also, don't forget some of the government websites such as O Net that have great information about different jobs and their responsibilities. This can be a great resource in your due diligence.

https://www.onetonline.org/

Lastly, do not pass up on just doing some web surfing and look up some local companies that might pique your interest. Look at their websites from the perspective that you want to bring value to them and see if you can craft a "sweet spot" that reflects your brand, your value proposition and your perspective of what you think their underserved need might be.

The world is full of "floating bubbles." Once you start looking aggressively, you will find them. Just be prepared to work with them and integrate them into your "sweet spot" development process. If you can nail this, you will always have opportunities.

Good luck!

NOW WHAT?

Career plan development activity—Either use the following examples from a successful marketing firm, or find your own job descriptions online, and then go through the process of documenting your brand, your personal value proposition and then how your personal "sweet spot" can be explored from pursuing one of these listed opportunities.

Project Manager:
- Review and manage Proposal Requests
- Manage trafficking and place orders for media buys
- Review and schedule newsletters
- Assign projects and set up time tracking software
- Check ads for errors and communicate necessary changes to the design team

Social Media Coordinator:
- Send out standard social media files and promotional material to partners each month
- Evaluate post promotion activities that are using social media
- Participate actively in promoting content to social media
- Demonstrate expert knowledge of all social media platforms

- Work with the team to develop strategy to use appropriate social media platforms for both internal use and client support

Digital Advertising Coordinator:
- Update specific client's websites
- Review common search teams and optimize search engine utilizations
- Monitor budget for digital advertising activities
- Managing all advertising and ensuring that renewals are processed in a timely manner
- Monitor new opportunities to use different media more effectively
- Confirm that every advertisement is running on a recurring basis
- Make necessary changes to internal home page
- Manage tracking sheets to be able to report project status to the clients
- Assist in the development of material for presentations to current and potential clients

Think about how you might articulate the value proposition in such a way that if you were to make connection with someone from this firm, it would be clear to them that you are a valuable resource regardless of whether or not, they have actually placed a job posting in the local career placement website.

Practice with this information and then go a step further and make an entry into your career plan development timeline to continue to practice this activity especially if you can tie it into an upcoming career fair or other activity that is being held on campus or at a local venue that fits your needs.

REFERENCES

Mapping your Unique Value: a Roadmap to Personal Branding, Washington State Chapter of the Urban and Regional Information Systems Association Conference—2014

10 Hot Job Titles that did not Exist 10 Years Ago, http://theundercoverrecruiter.com/top-job-titles-didnt-exist-5-years-ago/

SECTION 4.

TELLING your STORY

INTRODUCTION

N ow comes the really fun stuff. You get to talk about yourself! Cool huh?

Actually, this is where a lot of the processes break down. You have gone through the process of understanding yourself and have developed a strong entrepreneurial mind-set, and you have a killer sweet spot. If you could just hire a marketing professional to develop your advertising campaign, you would be all set.

Unfortunately it does not work that way. You are your own marketing manager, and you must learn to tell your story in a compelling and engaging way. We all watch advertisements that make us want to purchase the product. You must be able to create the same kind of promotional strategies.

Again, do not despair. You can do it. You just need to take the time to get clear about your story and then pay attention to the media you use to convey it to the public.

There are three ways that you tell your story. One is using the written word. The second is taking advantage of the opportunities provided via social media and the third option is when you are simply talking with someone either in a casual conversation or in a more structure environment, such as an interview.

We devote an entire chapter to each of those three media so that you can become a seasoned and effective marketing manager for your own version of I Inc.

9

Developing Written Tools

Let's do a brief recap. We have been working on developing an entrepreneurial mind-set in our career planning. As entrepreneurs, we constantly look for the value we bring to the market, are in touch with the potential competition, and are active participants in an ongoing process to ensure our skills and abilities are in sync with what is needed in the market. When we are faced with conflicting priorities, we are disciplined in our approach, strive to make decisions based on an entrepreneurial mind-set, and continuously update our personal database consistent with this approach.

Sound about right? If so, then we are ready to start digging into some basics. However, if you are still stuck on any of those concepts, you might want to revisit the previous section and give it some further thought. As we journey through the rest of the book, we will consistently approach the items from the entrepreneurial mind-set. If you are not comfortable with that approach, it would be better to back up and review the material until you are comfortable.

Since you have continued to read, I assume you are reasonably comfortable with the idea of approaching your career-planning process with an entrepreneurial mind-set. If that is the case, then our first tool to explore is the resume. To prepare to do this, go back and reacquaint yourself with your personal value proposition.

RESUME

You cannot visit a bookstore or Amazon and review career books without finding literally hundreds of resources on how best to create a resume. However, I will attempt to cut through a lot of the jargon regarding resumes and keep it really simple. The facts is, a recruiter will spend twenty to thirty seconds reading your resume. That is it! Twenty to thirty seconds. Try to see how much of this page you can read in that much time. And then put yourself in the recruiter's place and imagine you have one hundred or more resumes you must read and will only follow up with those that meet your expectations.

Recruiters simply have too much to do to study your resume and look for subtle nuances or try to interpret what you really mean when you say you are resourceful or hardworking. Since they give your resume such a brief review, if you try to make it cute, give it fancy script, or employ some other desperate attempt to make it unique, it will probably get rejected. Think about what recruiters do. They have been asked to screen hundreds of resumes and identify potential candidates to put in front of hiring managers. When recruiters forward a resume to a hiring manager, they are putting their own personal stamp of approval on the resume. If you were a recruiter, would you forward a resume with cute expressions or fancy script, or would you forward the resume that succinctly describes the value the candidate brings to the position? I believe you would go with the second option, and it is the one most recruiters choose in their review processes.

Recruiters also want to know why you did something that you include in your resume. If you change jobs frequently, include content to explain why. If you have a history of doing several different types of jobs, be sure it is obvious to the recruiter why you did so. You want to tell your personal story, and that means you want to be able to explain why you did things during that story.

RECRUITERS INITIALLY SCAN RESUMES LOOKING FOR REASONS TO REJECT YOU, NOT TO HIRE YOU

The bottom line is, your resume has to be flawless, easy to read, crystal clear in its delivery of the value you bring, and effective in telling your story—and do so in twenty seconds of reading time! Think like an entrepreneur. If you were going to devise a flyer that would attract people to your product or service, you would design it in such a way that it would be easy to read, clearly communicate the value of the product or service, and clearly communicate what the reader needs to do to participate in the program.

It is the same thing with a resume. It should be one page if possible. If you cannot say it in one page, you do not know yourself as well as you should, and you certainly are not able to clearly articulate the value you bring. Remember, even though a resume will include content from your past, it is not about your past. It is about your future! It is about what you can do for that employer. It is about the skills, knowledge, and track record you have established that make you valuable in the future. Too many people want to make it a laundry list of everything they have done to date. When you do that, you ask recruiters to sort through everything and decide what is important to them. You have to help them if they are going to make the decision you desire, in twenty seconds. If you try to use the laundry list approach, it is tantamount to a small company creating a flyer with several pages that list everything the company has done under the belief that a customer will sort through it and tell the company what they want. It will not work for a company, and it will not work for you.

Also, remember that a resume does not get you a job. It gets you an interview. It is a one-page flyer of your most significant abilities that are valuable to that employer and will encourage a recruiter to contact you and/or forward your resume to a hiring manager. We will discuss other tools you can use to tell your personal story in a more comprehensive manner, but trying to get it all on a resume is not the answer.

Here is a summary of the resume development process:

1. Think like an entrepreneur.
2. Keep it to one page if possible, two at the most.
3. Be absolutely certain there are no typos or grammatical errors. (Did you ever see a typo on a flyer? If you did, what did you think of that company?)
4. Make sure your contact information is clear and professional.

5. Include tangible examples of work you have done, and be sure to include the quantified outcomes, when possible, that have occurred as a result of your work.

Like I said, there are hundreds of books on how to create a resume. If you do not have one handy, you can download a guide from the internet or get one from a library or bookstore. However, what is more important than the actual form you choose for the resume is that you approach it from an entrepreneurial mind-set and sell yourself.

Of course, if you are selling something, you need to know who is willing to buy it. An entrepreneur will know the answer to that question. You must be able to address it; hopefully, a lot of what we covered earlier in the book will help you with this pursuit.

Also, remember that a resume is a necessary but not sufficient instrument for a viable career strategy. When you focus predominately on the resume and marginalize all of the other content we cover in this book, you are at a serious disadvantage in today's job market. It is one piece of the puzzle. An important one, but one nonetheless and it has to fit into your entire career search strategy.

As you pull your resume together, you may wonder if it hits the key points you think a given employer would want. Here is a fun activity that can help you get a sense for what is being communicated via your resume. There is actually a very helpful web page called Wordle. Go back to the entrepreneurial mind-set. If you were an entrepreneur trying to get people to buy your product or service, you would have two or three key value ideas you wanted your flyer to represent. You must do the same thing with your resume. Think of those two or three key words that reflect the essence of what you want people to think about you. Write them down. Then, once you have them, work on your resume. When you finally get it completed, go to the Wordle website and follow the instructions to create a word map of your resume. The outcome is actually a stylized word map that shows the most important key words in your document.

The following map was created when I put the Gettysburg Address into the application. We all know about Lincoln's speech and how it touched the soul of a nation divided. There can be no substitute for reading and reflecting on the

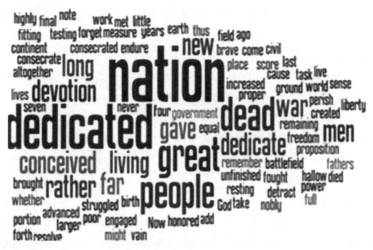

FIGURE 9.1. RESULT OF SUBMITTING THE GETTYSBURG ADDRESS INTO THE WORDLE.NET APPLICATION.

speech, but the above map does give you a sense of the breadth and depth of the words he chose as well as the key thoughts that are covered in the speech. The nation was at war, and its survival was being challenged. However, in the face of this great tragedy, people were still dedicated to the preservation of the nation. Those two words, *nation* and *dedicated*, capture the essence of the speech. They were closely followed by *dead* and *great people*, which spoke to the pain of war but also hope for the future.

I had a student once who wanted his resume to convey his willingness to take risks, be open to ideas, and be willing to take on new roles and stretch his abilities. We fed his resume into Wordle and received a word map that emphasized things like being a good manager, being meticulous, and being very strong at paying attention to details. These are certainly not bad things, but they were not what he wanted to communicate to potential recruiters. The point is that you may be thinking one thing, but your message may come across totally differently. Using Wordle is one way to test the congruency of your message.

Another approach is simply to ask someone you trust to read your resume and give you feedback on the key elements. Regardless of the approach, be sure to write down what you think those key elements are ahead of time and then use one of these approaches to validate what you have included in your resume. By the way, this is another form of how your personal brand is communicated to those who read your resume.

The reason I am focusing on the idea of elements is twofold. First, the entrepreneur knows what his or her key elements are. You must have the same mind-set. Second, remember that the recruiter will only take twenty seconds to read your resume. He or she is going to do a lot of summarizing and assuming in that time. You must ask yourself: "What are the key elements the recruiter will retain from the review of the resume?"

The bottom line is, keep it simple. Think like an entrepreneur. View your resume as your personal one-page flyer that must work when you are not there. Be sure it is flawless and use a professional format that is easily read and will encourage the recruiter to pass it on to the hiring manager.

HOW RECRUITERS USE RESUMES

Remember, a recruiter is not going to spend a lot of time doing a deep dive into your resume. They want to be able to tell in 10–15 seconds whether or not you are a match for the job and if they should forward you to the next step in the process.

In order to improve your chances of not being cut during the first pass, it is important for you to have a general idea of what is happening when a recruiter is looking at your resume. First off, they are looking for reasons to reject you, not hire you. I know that sounds harsh, but a recruiter may receive over 100 resumes, to get it down to a list of 5 that they want to present to a hiring manager, who will ultimately hire one person. That is a ratio of 100:1, and in many cases it is even worse.

Like I mentioned earlier, when a recruiter forwards your resume to the hiring manager, the recruiter is putting their personal stamp of approval on your resume, and they have to feel relatively confident that you will impress the hiring manager. If there is any doubt or if they are not able to clearly see how you can bring value to the company or worse case, they see typos or poor grammar in your resume, then it is going to get rejected.

Also, do not believe that they are going to comb through your resume looking for relevant examples of how you can do the work. You want it to be explicit and tied to the job for which you are applying. Also, it is very important that you have made some kind of contact within the company to help the recruiter make the decision to send you forward. If you have not done anything in the way of networking or making connections outside of the formal resume process, the odds are stacked against you.

Bottom line, accept the fact that recruiters are only taking a short time to review your resume, will reject you for even the slightest error, will not be patient if it is not clear how you bring value and are more receptive to an application of they have some other information, perhaps from a contact within the company, that is helping them make the decision to send you forward.

HOW TO MAKE YOUR RESUME POP!

Now, I am not going to tell you to do a key word search and be sure that you have included specific words in your resume so that it will not get rejected by the electronic scanner. By the way, that is a technique that recruiters have put in place because they are totally overwhelmed with the number of resumes they get through the internet. This fact is part of the reason we say that the system is broken. If you are focused on ensuring that you put key words into your resume, you have violated the key principles that we have been discussing in this book. Namely make some connections, do some informational interviews, reach out and network with people and get someone looking for your resume on the inside. Doing that is probably the best way to circumvent the initial high volume scanning and at least get a recruiter to look at your resume.

But that approach alone is not enough to make it pop. You want to include tangible, hard hitting examples of the work you have done that the recruiter and hiring manager can relate to and can see how you can bring value to their company. We have included a couple of resume templates to give you an idea of how to format a resume but I want to take a minute and talk about how to include activity that you have done that is relevant to the potential job for which you are applying.

Do not list everything that you have done in your previous job. When you include a laundry list of all of your activities, you are telling the hiring manager that you are not sure what is valuable for them and are asking them to sort through the list. Also, this type of list is more descriptive of what you have don't and not what you have accomplished.

You want to include three elements in your examples of what you have done. Start with an action verb that is strong such as *implemented, developed, trained, produced,* etc. *Coordinate* is OK but is a little weak, so try to make it a verb that is very easy for someone to visualize that you did.

The second part is the recipient of the action. *Developed a new program* or *trained the new staff,* etc. Again, write it in a way that the recruiter can clearly see who or what was the recipient of the action.

The third part is the tangible outcome. Be critical of yourself at this step and ask yourself the question, "So What?" If nothing significant happened as a result of what you did, then you probably do not want to include it. Ask yourself what happened as a result of what you did. Did you develop a new program that improved customer satisfaction or did you train the new team in order to reduce errors in the production cycle?

Three things: *action, recipient, outcome*—and make them hard hitting and your resume will pop!

Outcomes are important in a resume and you want to be able to focus on what happened as a result of what you did. The outcomes should be positive so that the hiring manager can get a feel for the idea that if you achieved those outcomes in your prior job, it is reasonable to assume that you could achieve similar outcomes in the new position.

Outcomes should be focused on how you had a positive impact on the customer, the team and/or the financial bottom line. You also want to include tangible outcomes when possible, so quantify them when you can.

The following three examples are weak when it comes to outcomes:

- Worked with businesses to carry out United Way fund-raising goals
- Helped accountants with various public accounting projects
- Developed marketing plans to promote concert series on campus

You may feel that these are adequate, and they are better than simply saying something like *raised funds* or *helped the accountants*, but they can be much better. Here are three examples that are much stronger. Notice the action verb, recipient of the action and tangible outcome:

- Partnered with more than 20 area businesses to raise $15,000 for United Way, exceeding the goal by 23%
- Assisted accountants with auditing $55,000 in account receivables for company's largest client
- Developed fully integrated marketing campaign distributed to 10,000 students, resulting in 12% increase in concert attendance

Be critical of what you include in the resume. Remember how quickly the recruiter or hiring manager will be reading it. Make it flawless in spelling and grammar and include some hard hitting, impactful examples of how you brought value to your old job and how you can bring value to the new opportunity. It is not rocket science, but it does take some effort and very close attention to detail. Good luck.

COMMON RESUME FORMATS

There are many different potential formats for your resume, but I want to include a couple for you to consider. One is a chronological resume, which basically describes what you have done in chronological order starting with the most recent work and then going backward. The second example is a functional resume. Once you get some decent experience, trying to use a chronological resume might not be the best thing for you. Instead, think about the top three or four things that you want to convey to an employer about your personal value, and then build those functional descriptions. For instance, if I were developing a resume, I might want an employer to know about my project management experience, my knowledge of financial controls, and my ability to develop new business opportunities. If I were to try to use a chronological resume, those points might get lost. But by listing them separately in a functional resume, I am able to focus attention on the skills that are most representative of my personal value proposition.

The key is to use the format that best serves you and communicates to an employer your personal value proposition in the most effective manner. I have included two examples to assist you in developing your resume. The first is a chronological resume, and the second is a functional resume.

Again, there are numerous resources online to help you with your resume, but be sure to take the time initially to decide on the message you want to share before you begin to develop your resume.

CHRONOLOGICAL RESUME

Public A. Student

(123) 456-7890

xxxxx@umich.edu

EDUCATION:

University of Michigan–Dearborn   Dearborn, MI

Bachelor of Business Administration   9/14–Present

Major: Financial Accounting and Reporting   GPA: 3.25   Expected Graduation: 12/17

Relevant Courses:

- Accounting
- Tax Accounting
- Asset Accounting
- Decision Science–Statistics
- Calculus
- Organizational Behavior

ACADEMIC PROJECTS:

The University of Michigan–Dearborn

- Developed and presented a proposal to help the College of Business, Internship Office migrate to a common student registration system
- Created a proposal to help the Accounting Aid Society more effectively schedule tax preparers with their clients

WORK EXPERIENCE:

Dunham's Sports Goods   Southgate, MI

Sales Associate   February 2014–Present

- Interact with approximately 25 customers per day, sharing product knowledge and personal advice in order to consistently maintain top sales figures
- Manage complaints and customer discrepancies to resolve problems, leading to increased customer satisfaction
- Prepare seasonal displays, designing store layout and item placement, driving sales for winter and summer seasons

Market Square   West Bloomfield, MI

Assistant Produce Manager   *May 2012–December 2013*

- Developed a coupon discount program working closely with a local marketing firm resulting in a 20% increase in sales
- Partnered with more than 20 area businesses to raise $15,000 for the United Way, exceeding the goal by 23%
- Conducted monthly and yearly inventory to prepare for future orders

SKILLS:

Computer Skills: Proficient in Microsoft Word, Excel, PowerPoint, Access, HTML, Visual Basic, and familiar with C++ programming

Languages: Able to interpret and present concepts in Arabic

FUNCTIONAL RESUME

Public A. Employee

(123) 456-7890

xxxxx@gmail.com

CORE COMPETENCIES

Project Management

- Led the successful implementation of new accounts receivable system for a global client
- Trained staff in the proper use of MS Project to balance the workload
- Helped develop new issue tracking procedure for internal operations

Financial Controls

- Implemented improved reporting procedures for our client in tracking their operations in foreign countries
- Developed and conducted a new training program for our company's interns
- Implemented a new cost-savings approach for our client that resulted in an improvement of their overall profit by 10% each year

New Business Development

- Built new client relationships with over 5 companies last year, resulting in new business of over $25 million in annual revenue
- Developed and implemented a new training program for our new college graduates in the areas of sales and new market development

EDUCATION:

University of Michigan–Dearborn	Dearborn, MI
Bachelor of Business Administration	Graduated 9/08
Major: Financial Accounting and Reporting GPA: 3.25	

WORK EXPERIENCE:

Capgemini	Detroit, MI
Division Vice President	8/12–Present
General Motors	Detroit MI
Account Manager	1/10–8/12

Deloitte   Southfield, MI
Project Manager   8/08–1/10

SKILLS:

<u>Project Management</u>: Proficient in MS Project and Proprietary Financial Management Packages, including SAP and People Soft
<u>Languages</u>: Fluent in Portuguese and Spanish

COVER LETTER

Traditional literature about careers and cover letters are pretty simple. In fact, I have come to learn that there are a lot of recruiters out there who do not even read cover letters. Nonetheless, you want yours to be well written, just in case someone decides to pick it up and read it. Also, the very act of creating the cover letter gives you one more chance to practice articulating your key values to the organization.

Think about a cover letter from the entrepreneurial mind-set. Whereas the resume can be compared to the marketing flyer, the cover letter can be thought of as the home page on your website. It needs to communicate who you are, why you are valuable, and what the next steps for the reader are if he or she is interested. You would include those elements on your home page if you were in business, and you should include the same concepts in your cover letter.

One difference from the home page metaphor is that a cover letter should be specifically addressed to an individual if possible. Sending something out addressed "To whom it may concern" is a major turn-off for most recruiters. If you are interested in the company, you must have done some research to understand how you can bring value to that firm. When you do the research, get the name and contact information for the person who will receive your letter.

Another word of caution, which also pertains to the website. Make certain that there are no grammatical errors or typos. If you look at a website and it has errors, you will probably go to the next potential resource. Again, remember that when it comes to cover letters and resumes, recruiters are looking for reasons to eliminate you. They might read one hundred cover letters and resumes to narrow the pool down to twenty candidates to call and narrow that down to ten for an initial interview so they can send three candidates to the hiring manager. It is a game of numbers, and you do not want to be a casualty. Never give them a reason to eliminate you from the process. Typos and poor grammar are the death of many job seekers, so pay attention to the details.

Consider getting a friend to proofread your resume or cover letter, or maybe even try reading the documents backward. When you read something backward, your mind does not know what is coming next, and so it will not fill in the correct word for you. Our minds are wonderful things, but they can actually do us a disservice in this case. I am sure you have seen examples of errors that are purposefully inserted in text to show how it works. Your mind is watching out for you and will fill in the word or correct the typo for you. This helps when you are trying to understand something, but it is terrible if you are trying to avoid a typo in an important document.

However you choose to do it, do not simply read the words and assume that you will catch the errors. While editing this book, I asked many of my colleagues to help proofread it; even so, there will probably be a few errors that slipped by. I see it all the time in books I read, but you do not want it in a resume or cover letter.

Regardless of the technique you use, take the time to make these documents flawless. It will pay dividends in the future.

The bottom line with cover letters is they need to have three sections: an introduction, a statement of your value for that specific company, and a statement of what the next steps are.

Begin by introducing yourself and explaining why you are sending the letter. Recruiters often have a myriad of jobs they are trying to fill, and if they get a letter without an explanation of what it is for, they will probably reject it.

Secondly, be sure to explicitly state why you are valuable for the given position. If they have posted a job description and you are replying to it, say how you are qualified in each of the critical areas listed in the job description. Address them in your letter in the same sequence as in the description. Make it really easy for the recruiter to put you in the follow-up pile instead of the reject pile.

Lastly, take as much responsibility for the next steps as possible so you can maintain some degree of control over the process. You can say you will follow up with a phone call or some other action to help keep the ball rolling. The more you can stay engaged, the more the recruiter will appreciate your interest and initiative. Don't go overboard and say you will call them every day, but do try to lay out what you feel the next steps should be in the process and end with a gracious close.

E-MAIL

We all use electronic forms of communication to stay in touch. In chapter 10 we will go into more detail about the types of social media communication that are available to you. However, we do need to make a brief comment about e-mail within the context of written communication.

The professional world revolves around the use of e-mail. It is hard to find a business leader who does not use it extensively and rely on it to stay abreast of what is happening in the professional world. As a result, businesses use it extensively in their hiring processes, so you should respect that fact and learn to use it effectively.

Some guidelines to consider in using e-mail include the following:

1. Keep up-to-date on your communication. You should never go longer than twenty-four hours before you respond. If you are going to be on vacation or away from the system, be sure to include an away message. Take the communication seriously and respond promptly.
2. Keep your communication professional. Address it properly and sign it with a professional salutation. Do not use expressions such as *hey* or *later* in your text. That is fine with friends, but keep the e-mail professional when you are communicating with potential employers.
3. Stay away from abbreviations such as *lol, omg*, and others that you might use in friendly texting.
4. Proofread it closely. Do not rely on the spell-checker to do the work for you. Be certain that the grammar is correct and there are no misspellings.
5. Try not to have several topics in one e-mail. A busy executive might only read the first part of the e-mail and might miss other topics. If you must include more than one item, use numbers or bullets to call attention to the fact that there is more than one topic in the e-mail.

The bottom line is to be thorough, professional, and respectful and stay on top of your e-mails. They will open doors for you, but they can also close them easily.

ADDITIONAL RESOURCES

As I mentioned earlier in this chapter, there are many resources that you can use to help create your resume. Remember, it is not the format but the content that is most important, but here are some places where you can get some help with the format if necessary.

https://www.myperfectresume.com/
https://www.resumehelp.com/
https://resumegenius.com

And if none of these fit your needs, simply do a Google search on resume templates and you will have all the help with the format that you can use.

NOW WHAT?

The most obvious place to start is with your resume. But before you do that, take a little time to do a skills inventory.

Take out a blank piece of paper, draw three vertical lines, and label the headings Skills, Under-served Need, and Personal Value Proposition. Then list eight to ten skills you currently possess that you feel are valuable to an employer. Then think about what we have discussed regarding under-served need and your personal value proposition; in each of those columns, place an X when that skill addresses an under-served need or will complement your personal value proposition. Take a look at the following table as an example.

Skills	Under-served Need	Personal Value Proposition
Project management	X	X
Excel		
Problem solving	X	X
Presentations		
Written communication	X	

Based on this table, the two skills (project management and problem solving) are fairly important in terms of both your sense of the under-served need and as part of your personal value proposition. If that were the case, then as you develop your resume, think about how you can include tangible examples of those two specific abilities.

You should develop a resume, and possibly even have a couple of different ones, but resist the temptation to make it a laundry list of what you have done. Think about the skills you bring to the job and also give serious thought to what is needed, and then use the resume to tell your personal story. Good luck.

Another possible action step is to check out different templates online for resumes and cover letters. However, if you do that, do not just accept them blindly. Look for formats that serve you but make sure that they convey your intended message and are easy to understand. Fancy fonts and hard-to-read documents will not score you any points with recruiters.

The last suggestion is to go back and read several e-mails you have recently sent to someone in an influential position. Take a critical look at each e-mail and see if you can find any typos or grammatical errors. Also, look for any terminology that is not absolutely professional. One mistake students make is to refer to their professors by their last names when talking about them with their friends. However, if they let that flow over and refer to the professor by just his or her last name in a correspondence, they are creating a serious error. If a professor has told you to use his or her first name, then by all means, do so. But if not, you should use a title before the last name. The same thing goes for contacting a business executive or someone else in a position of authority. These individuals deserve your respect, and unless they have advised you to call them by a more casual name, you should refrain from doing so.

Take a look at a few e-mails and be critical. Learn what you have done incorrectly and make sure you do not make the same errors going forward.

Dig out your career plan template and make a commitment to complete one or two items that fall under the written part of telling your story. It might be to review your resume, or have a career counselor do it or it might be simply to write a cover letter and ask someone for an informational interview. Make a couple commitments to get the ball rolling and follow through.

Regardless of the written document you produce, you must be certain that it is flawless and that you are proud to share it with others. It takes a little effort to do, so but it will pay off in many ways going forward.

REFERENCES

Wordle. 2014. http://www.wordle.net.

10

Capitalizing on Social Media Strategies

INTRODUCTION

Obviously, the job market has changed significantly in the past few years. We all know that we can now connect with anyone on the planet in a matter of seconds. This connectivity has given us a whole new way to participate in the job search. It does have its challenges, but the opportunities are too significant for you not to take the time to master the tools at your disposal.

In this chapter, we will cover some of the more common tools such as Facebook, Twitter, and LinkedIn, along with the ideas of creating an electronic portfolio and a video resume that you can use in a variety of settings.

However, the key is to always keep in mind what message you are sharing. Because of the near instantaneous communication provided by social media, it is important that you think through your message and then confirm that your approach will serve your purpose. However, do not let that dissuade you from jumping in and taking advantage of these tools. They are a must in today's job quest.

FACEBOOK

It is fascinating and informative to watch how other people use this tool. I have seen posts from senior executives letting people know that they are heading to a conference or engaging in a new business venture. I have seen people post about a political topic in which they are especially interested, and I have seen people post pictures of their family, pets, or even friends engaging in enjoyable activities. Unfortunately, I have also seen posts that do not serve the individual who decided to send a message to the world about a recent activity that was less than flattering. Again, do not be reluctant to use the tool, but do give some consideration as to who will be viewing it and what message do you want to send.

I recently had the opportunity to post an announcement on Facebook, and I came to realize that there is not just one way or one topic that is appropriate. I think that is part of the beauty of this tool. It is your personal tool to communicate with whomever you want, whenever you want, about whatever subject you want to share. Again, think about the power this provides and take advantage of that power.

There are the normal reminders about not posting anything that would be offensive or would cast you in an unfavorable light with a potential employer. However, even that word of caution can be subject to interpretation. The bottom line is to simply think before you post and be sure that you are proud of what you are posting. You do not need to feel that you have to conform. Be proud of your personal preferences, but always remember that you are sharing them with the entire world.

Recruiters will do an online search of you before they invite you to interview. In fact, it does not hurt if you know the recruiter's name and do the same with him or her. It is all about having more access to information, and the more you can take advantage of that fact in a meaningful way, the better equipped you will be for today's market.

Jump into Facebook if you have not done so already. Explore the different ways you can communicate. Build your friends list and use it to improve your understanding of people in your life as well as to help people know more about you in those areas in which you want to share.

TWITTER

Twitter can actually provide you with three valuable abilities. The first is access to a wealth of information that knowledgeable people share through the system. The trick is learning about who is knowledgeable and providing valuable content for you to read.

Begin by following experts in your area of interest. Take the time to check out their posts. Use that information to expand your personal knowledge base of different subjects. You can remove or skip over the ones that you do not feel are valuable. But use it to gain insight. There are an unlimited number of resources for you to access through this method.

The second feature is that Twitter gives you a way to share your perspective when you have sufficient expertise to post your own thoughts on a certain topic. You do not need to be a well-seasoned expert, but if you are going to share something for other people to read, give some thought to its relevance and interest. You can post all sorts of things, but if no one is reading them, they are not having any kind of impact.

You can either repost someone else's thought or you can post your own perspective on a given topic. The whole idea of doing this is to build your brand equity. You can communicate to your followers that you have a degree of expertise in a given subject and people should want to read what you have to say. This feature is probably the most difficult to develop but can certainly be valuable in helping you further develop and communicate your personal brand.

Twitter can give you access to knowledge that you might not otherwise have been able to gain. It can also help you enhance your brand and make you better known in your career field. Take advantage of it, use it wisely, and it will help with your career pursuits.

The last feature, which can actually be a lot of fun and will give you all sorts of ways to connect, is actually participating in a chat. When you send a tweet, it is published for all to see, but if you precede the tweet with a hashtag expression, it will filter what you send to and receive from other users who are using that specific hashtag. For instance, if you are setting up a chat, either choose the unique hashtag or find out from the moderator what hashtag will be used. A hashtag is any unique expression that has the # sign at the beginning. For instance, if you use the expression #ncdachat and told others you would be using that hashtag at a certain time, they could join you for the chat simply by using that hashtag at the start of their tweet.

There are chat rooms that cover just about any topic. You can do a Google search on Twitter chat directories and get a list of directories you can search for specific topics of interest. Your own school's career center might even be using this tool.

The key is to explore and look for chat rooms that are of interest to you. After you have participated in some, you might want to moderate your own chat. Again, it is a way to gain access to topics in which you are interested and also to give you a chance to post your ideas. The idea of using the hashtag simply helps narrow the field of who you chat with.

There is no wrong way to do it. You can follow experts, post your own observations, participate in chat rooms, and even moderate your own chats. Jump in and experiment. You have the world to discover and really nothing to lose.

LINKEDIN

LinkedIn is clearly the most important social media tool you can use in your career quest. Almost every recruiter I speak with not only is on LinkedIn but uses it as a primary tool in sourcing candidates. It is the professional social media networking tool, and you should take the time to build your profile and use the features effectively.

Building an effective LinkedIn profile will take time. Do not try to do it in fifteen or twenty minutes. Take as much time as you need to review the different components, make notes about what you want to cover, and pull the information together to help you in your quest.

To start your profile, upload a nice picture of yourself. Do not use one that has been cropped from a much larger picture and do not use a selfie. The cropped on will look grainy and will convey to the reader that you are not taking the time to do this right. A selfie is way too casual and again, conveys the sense that you are not taking the time to create a professional profile. Your picture does not have to be a professional portrait, but get a nice head shot of you looking into the camera and, preferably, smiling will go a long way. And get it close enough so that viewers can see you. The idea is to let the recruiter get a feel for who you are, and it starts with the picture.

The second thing to consider is the headline. Too many students simply use something like "Accounting student, looking for an internship" or something similar. That kind of headline will not separate you from the pack. You want to use a headline that is unique to you. You want something that will stand out and can be part of what makes you special. A more appropriate headline might be "Emerging accounting professional, solid problem solver and capable of helping you manage your financial transactions" or something like that. The headline is the start of your personal pitch, so take a little time and give it some thought.

Next comes the summary. Here is where you can take a paragraph or two and summarize who you are and the value you bring to an employer. But do not overdo it. One or two brief paragraphs at the most will serve you very well. This is not just an opportunity to write about yourself, but rather to take your skills and abilities and translate them into a statement that describes how you can help a given company. Remember, you are marketing yourself, so use the opportunity to write a summary statement that markets your abilities. It should be longer than one sentence and no more than a couple of small to medium-sized paragraphs. In the summary section, you can include a link to your Twitter account or other personal web pages you have created. It will give readers even more things to review about you if they are so inclined.

The whole idea of using LinkedIn is that it can be so much more than just a sheet of paper. You can bring it to life with videos, blogs, pictures, and other content to make it interesting. Take the time, give it some thought, think about what you want to include, and then pull together a summary that sets the stage for the entire profile. And after you have developed your summary, take a critical look at it and think about what a recruiter would say if he or she read it. Again, take the time to do it right.

If you are still in college then I recommend you include the education section next. You can adjust the sequence of the different sections, so give some thought to what you want to come first and what you want to follow. A way to think about the sequence is to include the most important items first and then let the less important topics go more toward the end of the profile. While you are still a student, your education experience is probably going to be more important and more relevant to a recruiter, but once you have graduated and gotten some experience, you can move the experience section in front of the education section. However, at this time, I recommend that you lead with your education right after the summary section. It should be one of your strongest selling points. List your university, your major, your expected graduation date, and some of the key courses you have taken that help make you more valuable. This section, along with most of the others, is subject to periodic review and update, so don't forget to do that as you work toward your career aspirations.

I would then include work experience, both paid and unpaid. This is where you can expand on the skills, knowledge, track record, and relationships that you have been developing. Again, be sure to frame the experiences in terms of how you helped the people, customers, and/or business processes wherever you worked.

Following the education section, you have the opportunity to list some skills. When you are starting your profile, I recommend you include at least five skills you feel you possess. LinkedIn has a fairly distinctive feature whereby people who connect with you can endorse you for the skills you possess. The system will send your contacts requests to see if they endorse you for the skills you have listed, so if you start with specific skills, you will tend to get endorsed on those skills.

One nice feature of this process is that over time, you will see your endorsements grow, and they will actually reflect what people think of you—also known as your personal brand. Check it out a few months after you build your profile and see what brand is emerging. You can edit it if you want, but pay attention to it. It is what people are saying about you, and that is valuable information.

Also include any honors or awards you have received as well as any significant projects you have completed. Again, make these meaningful. If they speak to your personal value proposition, you should definitely include them. However, do not just add items to fill up the profile. Add content that is meaningful and helps differentiate you in the market.

FINISHING TOUCHES

We discussed references and recommendations earlier in general in chapter 6. You might want to go back and review that content and apply it to your approach to ask for these to support your LinkedIn presence. Furthermore, you might want to seek out some professional people who can speak to the value you bring and can articulate why you are different, and ask them for a recommendation.

And don't forget to include any organizations in which you were active. Student organizations that focus on professional development are great items to include, but do not just say you were a member of the organization. Say a little about the value you brought to that organization. Just listing the name of a professional or student organization on your resume does not look that special. What does look good is stating how you were able to contribute to the people, customers, and/or business challenges associated with that organization.

One more thing to consider before you declare your profile complete: you must decide how much of it you want to make completely public. The way LinkedIn works is, if you connect with someone, they are able to see your profile. However, what about all those recruiters and other contacts you want to reach? This is where the public version of your profile comes in. When you are in the mode of editing your profile, you can create a link that contains items you want everyone to be able to see. You can even name the public link to be more reflective of your personal brand and include it on your business card. The key is that you are able to control what the casual observer will be able to see about you, so be sure that what is being shown captures your personal brand.

I have seen some wonderful LinkedIn profiles that I know are garnering a lot of interest from recruiters, but I see a lot more that are hastily prepared and are nothing more than a placeholder. Take the time to do it right. It is probably the most critical component of your social media strategy, so invest the required time and be professional.

VIDEO RESUMES

A fairly recent and innovative approach in the world of career development is the use of a video resume. One advantage of using this technique is that it gives you the chance to demonstrate your technological adeptness. However, you want it to be appropriate; so, depending on the target market, different technological solutions might work better. Give it some thought and use it wisely, but it does give you the chance to demonstrate your ability instead of just talking about it.

Video resumes can be candid and creative. You will probably not have the ability to use a teleprompter, so your dialog must flow smoothly and naturally. That can be a challenge for some people, so prepare yourself to make a few recordings before you nail it.

Use of a video resume has the ability to set you apart, but you obviously want to use good judgment and keep it professional. Again, use it as a tool to tell your story if it serves you. Do not use it just because you can, but rather because it gives you the opportunity to present your skills and abilities in a way that you feel strengthens your personal value proposition.

ELECTRONIC PORTFOLIOS

Electronic portfolios are exciting and becoming a key component in the recruiting process. To create one, identify different files that are representative of your personal story and then craft a brief message with each file to pull them together into a coherent message.

This technique enables you to document significant accomplishments by using different forms of electronic media to enhance interest in what you have done and make a lasting impression on the viewer. It gives you the chance to go way beyond what can be communicated via a resume or cover letter and can get into much more detail, in an interesting and engaging manner, than can be communicated via a sheet of paper. It also gives you a great opportunity to sort through the variety of activities and accomplishments in your history and to create a compelling story to share with a potential employer.

If you were applying for a job as a dress designer, you would have a portfolio of the work you have done. You would show your creativity and innovation in your portfolio design and would want it to entice potential customers to buy a dress from you. The electronic portfolio is nothing more than a collection of accomplishments, generally in a digital format, that tell your personal story and highlight the value of your personal contribution. Through this technique, you can create something that focuses on the unique value you can bring to a company.

If you are new to this concept, you should do a little research and come up with a way to create your portfolio. There are several options available to you in this regard. One is to use the capability that is provided via LinkedIn. You can use this feature in LinkedIn without having to pay for the advanced features, and the portfolio option can be accessed simply via the personal profile feature in LinkedIn.

A second option is to contact a company like Optimal Resume and arrange for an individual registration. This might be a little problematic because these companies tend to offer subscriptions to colleges and universities and generally are not involved with individual purchases. However, if you feel that the LinkedIn option is not for you, you certainly can do some research and seek out a company that will provide you with access to an electronic portfolio feature at a reasonable price. And don't forget to check with your university; it may have a subscription with a company that will support you creating your own personal electronic portfolio.

The third option is simply to create your own web page. Be sure you have a clear focus on creating something that showcases your skills and abilities as well as your track record relative to the kinds of positions you are looking for. Your web page must be every bit as professional as a small business's website and should not include general information that you might post to Facebook or some other social media site. This website needs to tell your story, say how you are valuable, and communicate why employers should consider you for their firm.

Research your options, decide on the tool you want to use, and get busy creating your electronic portfolio. As you prepare to create your portfolio, get out that entrepreneur mind-set, identify the three or four key attributes that separate you from the competition, and then look for different types of electronic media to help you tell your story.

Remember, the electronic portfolio is not a dumping ground for everything electronic that you have and can share with the world. It has to be developed with strategic intent. For instance, if the three things you want to communicate to potential employers are strong project management skills, solid presentation skills, and outstanding problem-solving skills, you should find examples of these three elements where you have been successful and decide how you want to represent them in your portfolio. Again, if you can use different types of media, the portfolio will be even more interesting. You might choose to include a project plan and a letter from a satisfied customer to show your project management abilities. You might include a YouTube video of a presentation you made recently to highlight the presentation skills dimension, and you could include a report you wrote outlining the different options of a particularly messy problem and how you went about solving it. Use the portfolio to craft your personal story in a compelling and interesting way.

Whatever personal traits and abilities you choose, you want to weave a story around them. Start with identifying the key attributes, followed by identifying forms of electronic media that support those attributes, and then finish the process by writing brief summaries of the different files in a way that tells the story of what makes you special and valuable.

Do not despair when you first try to do this. Most people are not in the habit of using this type of tool, and they may struggle to figure out what files to include. Regardless of how you choose to do it, get started pulling the files together. In fact, you may not have everything you need at this time to publish your portfolio in a way that satisfies your expectations, and that is certainly OK. If you get started and identify areas where there are holes in your portfolio, you can document the work you are currently doing that will add to the portfolio over time.

ALL OF THESE TOOLS REQUIRE A PROCESS FOCUS, NOT A SINGULAR EVENT FOCUS

Actually, all these tools are ongoing works in progress. As your abilities change, your experiences will grow, and your track record will expand. At the same time, changes will constantly be occurring in the marketplace in terms of what is valuable. Through this ongoing process, you should be continuously updating these documents in order to remain relevant. The electronic portfolio technique gives you the chance to get started with what you have now. You can then update it with relevant accomplishments and remove content that becomes obsolete. All the while you will be maintaining a strong sense of the value you bring to the marketplace at any given time.

ADDITIONAL RESOURCES

LinkedIn has actually created the absolutely best reference for you to use in building your profile. Take a look at the following link and review the videos and other resources. Be sure to seek out the checklist for creating your own profile. It is specific and valuable and will give you the guidance you need to create a powerful profile. Good Luck!

https://students.linkedin.com/

NOW WHAT?

If you have not yet made the plunge into social media, do a little exploring so that you are familiar with some of the options. Talk with your friends, compare experiences, and make the commitment that you will be a player in this space.

Specifically, here are some options:

1. Build your LinkedIn profile. Follow the suggestions I laid out in this chapter and take the time to develop a professional profile in LinkedIn. Take a look at the following link and use what it offers: https://students.linkedin.com/.

2. Experiment a little with Twitter. See if you can find some interesting people to follow. Begin to retweet interesting topics and use it to share your insight into different ideas. Check out some Twitter directories by doing a Google search or take a look at the following link, http://chatsalad.com/, and find some chats that are of interest to you.

3. Use Facebook or whatever other social media tool works for you to communicate with your friends. Even Facebook can be used to propagate ideas or gain support for a cause. Use it wisely and be sure that whatever you post you would feel free sharing with everyone on the planet, because it just might happen.

4. Definitely take some time to develop an electronic portfolio. You can do this within LinkedIn or by creating your own web page or even signing up for service with companies like Optimal Resume. Your university may even have a subscription with a software package that will allow you to develop an electronic portfolio. The value of creating one is that it helps you articulate your personal value proposition even if no one ever looks at it. But they will.

5. Take a look at some video resumes that currently exist. Do a search on the internet for "video resumes," and you will find several different formats. And who knows, one might actually be of interest to you.

6. And before you finish this chapter, be sure to visit your career plan and identify a couple of things that you can do in the short term to beef up your social media presences and create a profile that you will be proud to show to anyone who is interested.

7. Lastly, develop a strategy for asking people to be a reference for you as well as who you could ask for a recommendation. Pull together some bullet points of the key elements in your personal value proposition so that when you ask someone for this type of help, you can give them the list of bullets.

REFERENCES

LinkedIn. "Student Jobs 101." 2015. https://students.linkedin.com.

ChatSalad. "The Real-Time Homepage for Twitter Chats." http://chatsalad.com.

11

Telling People about Your True Value

NETWORKING

The main coverage of this topic is in chapter 6, but it bears some further review simply because it is so important in how you build meaningful and valuable relationships. If you know anybody who is in business for themselves, it is safe to assume that you know someone who is good at networking. This is how new business relationships are developed. As an entrepreneur, you have to make connections and tell people about your value. And as a career development strategist using an entrepreneurial mind-set, it is the same thing.

There are different estimates ranging from 70 percent to 90 percent of jobs that never make it to the want ads. Most jobs get filled before they ever make it to the street. And for those that do make it to the want ads, most are for entry-level and lower-skilled jobs. It you want a shot at any kind of professional job, you have to network. It is a simple as that.

Everybody says the same thing. Networking is important. We all accept that it is, give lip service to its importance, and then, when we go to an event, hang out with our friends because that is our comfort zone. Don't do that! When you go to a networking event, network! Meet people you did not know before the event. Find out what they do, what interests them, what they have done in order to be successful. People like to talk about themselves. You can get the conversation going by simply introducing yourself and asking people what they do.

On the other hand, they may ask you the same thing, so you do must be prepared. Your preparation comes in the form of what has been called an "elevator speech." An elevator speech is roughly thirty seconds long and describes you, your unique values, and why someone might be interested in talking more with you and learning about what you are good at doing.

I often find that when students work on their elevator speech, they want to focus on the fact they are graduating from a prestigious university or with a specific major. You can certainly include those elements in your speech, but they should only take eight to ten seconds of the overall speech. The elevator speech clearly states how you are unique and how you bring value to the marketplace. Simply saying you graduated from a prestigious university will not sufficiently differentiate you from others in the job market. You must identify what makes you unique and what value you bring to the market.

Again, go back to the previous sections about the three attributes that characterize you. Those would make a great starting point for your elevator speech. Maybe something like this would work, based on the earlier example: "Hi, my name is Cameron Martin. I am a recent graduate from the University of Michigan. I have found that I love project management. It gives me the opportunity to deliver value to customers, engage in public speaking, and tackle some pretty messy problems that have turned out to be quite successful. I guess you might think of me as a strong project manager with a flair for communication while also being willing to tackle the tough challenges." That actually takes twenty seconds to recite in a meaningful way.

Take the time to write your elevator speech. Practice it so that it flows off your tongue and use it to explore other areas of interest as you watch people respond to your speech. This point is important. If people respond in a way that shows a lack of interest, then your speech needs work. On the other hand, if it perks up their ears and they want to learn more, you are making great progress!

You want it to sound spontaneous while also being authentic and believable. Don't make it sounds like you are reading it off a sheet of paper. Own it! Make it about you and your personal interests and values. You need to practice it until it flows naturally, and once you have it nailed, you will use it again and again when you meet someone new.

One technique I use is to print the triangle referenced in this book on the back of my business card. When I meet someone, I give a brief introduction to what I do; then as the opportunity presents itself, I give the person my card, show them the back, and use the image as a visual aid to help me tell my story.

Use whatever approach is comfortable for you. Watch other people and see how they do it. Borrow ideas from people you feel are effective in presenting their elevator speeches. Everyone is doing it. Some folks are masters, and it is a great idea to learn from them and use their approach in your delivery. Again, just make sure it is truly yours, and it will be successful.

Another advantage of having an elevator speech prepared is that you will be much more confident when you meet people. You have something to say. You are not trying to avoid people but rather are looking for opportunities to practice your speech. That puts you into a totally different state of mind and is consistent with the idea of approaching networking events with an entrepreneurial mind-set.

The thing to remember is that networking is supposed to be a common and casual occurrence. It is how people get together to make things happen. However, it can also be a little intimidating the first few times you try it. Here are some simple steps I compiled from different resources that will help you with the effort.

Learn how to **break the ice**. Keep it simple. You can just introduce yourself and ask something about why the other person is at the event. It does not need to be elaborate and really should only be a conversation starter. Break the ice in a simple and direct way and then see where it goes from there.

Get **warmed up**. You would not go into a ball game without stretching a little. Maybe take a few practice swings. Get a feel for the bat, club, or whatever you are using. The same thing applies to a networking event. Take a little time and get a feel for the event. Maybe talk to a few people at random. You may even get your motor running a little by chatting with the person handing out the name cards, or the bartender, or a waiter. The key is to get comfortable hearing your voice. There may be one or two key people you want to connect with at the event. Don't feel that you have to jump in and go to them directly. Talk with some of the other folks. It will ease your nerves and make you feel more confident when you do reach out to your key target.

Be aware of your **body language**. It is argued that more than 93% of communication is nonverbal. You want to give off a positive impression. One way of doing this is to avoid crossing your arms, since that tends to convey resistance to the ideas being discussed. Also, be sure to maintain a smile and positive image. When you speak with someone, maintain eye contact. If that makes you feel uncomfortable, you can just look at the bridge of the other person's nose. The person cannot tell that you are not looking at his or her eyes, and it is a way around looking directly at people if that makes you nervous. However, it is important to get to the point that you can look at people's eyes since they will tell you things also. Remember the 93% nonverbal factor. It goes both ways, and you must be able to tune in to it as much as others tune in to the messages you are sending.

Ask **great questions**. People love to talk about themselves. If you can ask people about what they do, what their current interests are, or where they see things going, you will go a long way toward getting the conversation started in a positive manner. I remember meeting the mayor of Detroit at a networking event, and I instantly asked him some questions about his college days. It turned out he had some connections with the university where I worked, and we had a nice conversation. Ask questions, let the other person talk about what is important to them, and then look for ways to make connections. It really does work!

Have fun. Again, networking is about making connections, and connections are how you get things done in business. You will have the opportunity to meet many interesting and successful people as you network in different settings. Once you get over any initial fear, you can let yourself go and have fun making connections with and learning about some interesting people.

INTERVIEWING SKILLS

Now comes the time for the proverbial rubber to meet the road. You have created a resume, a cover letter, and possibly a dynamic electronic portfolio that all tell your story based on the attributes you first identified in your personal value proposition. You are ready for prime time! You have been engaged in several net-working events, and at least one has paid off. You have been invited to interview for a position with a firm that does the kind of work that interests you, and you clearly can speak to the potential value you would bring to the firm.

Remember, you are an entrepreneur—or at least, you think like one. You have a valuable product or service to offer: you! You are looking for a good match between what you bring and what an employer values.

Interviewing is not about trying to guess the correct answers. Rather, it is about doing your homework on employers, knowing the value you can bring to them, and then discussing the prospects of you being successful in their specific environment. Interviewing is not a test; it is more like going on a date. You want to know if they are a good match for you, and they want to know if you are a good match for them.

That said, there are some great techniques to use to help improve the chances of you and an employer making a good choice in the process.

BEFORE THE INTERVIEW

RESEARCH THE ORGANIZATION

There is no excuse for not knowing about a company, with all the resources we have available to us via the internet. In order for you to talk about the value you bring, you must have done some research. Nothing will turn a recruiter off faster that not knowing anything about the company or why you are good for it. Do your homework!

PREPARE YOUR INTERVIEW OUTFIT

Dress "business professional" if the position is for a professional environment. You might be able to be more casual once you get to work, but be professional for the interview. A lot of recruiters have told me that if the candidate does not make the effort to present themselves in a professional manner, they assume the person is not really interested or committed to the job, so they pass on taking that person to the next step in the process. Err on the side of being professional. You can never be too professional, especially in the early stages of the selection process.

ASSEMBLE YOUR INTERVIEWING MATERIALS

Come prepared with copies of your resume, a list of references, a sense of the questions that you want to ask, and general information on the company. Be sure to be prepared to ask questions. Recruiters use this as a significant measure of an individual's interest and commitment to the position. Be prepared to ask questions about the company, where it is heading, and how you can help make it successful. These are not questions about what is served in the dining room or if there is ample employee parking. You want to ask questions that convey a clear sense that you want to learn more about what the company does, what challenges it faces, and how you can help bring value to those challenges.

PRACTICE INTERVIEWING

Use software packages to practice interviewing, if they are available to you, or do mock interviews through career services groups if you are on a university campus. However, if none of these are available, maybe you can ask a friend who knows about interviewing to let you practice with him or her. Do not go into the interview completely cold! Take some time to practice answering questions. Think about what you will say, and again, think like an entrepreneur and practice giving answers that convey the value that you bring to the organization. Think of the employer as a potential client and focus on solving his or her problems.

ON THE DAY OF THE INTERVIEW

ARRIVE EARLY

Don't show up too early, because that will lead to priority conflicts for the interviewer, but get there ten to fifteen minutes before the interview. It will give you a chance to relax, collect your thoughts, and then go into the interview with a professional demeanor.

TURN OFF YOUR CELL PHONE AND GET RID OF GUM OR CANDY

The last thing you want is your phone going off in the middle of the interview. However, if you forget to turn it off and someone calls you, do not answer it. Let it roll into voice mail or simply reject the call and then turn the phone off.

LEAVE THE COLOGNE OR PERFUME AT HOME

It is not a date! You do not want to load up on the perfume. Many people have a negative reaction to cologne or perfume, and the last thing you want is for the recruiter to be getting a headache and wanting to get you out of the office as soon as possible.

BE COURTEOUS TO EVERYONE YOU MEET

Employers often ask the receptionist or other people who come in contact with you what their reaction to you is. You don't need to be paranoid, but simply treat everyone respectfully. This is good advice regardless of whether you are on an interview or not.

GREET THE INTERVIEWER WITH A FIRM HANDSHAKE AND INTRODUCE YOURSELF

There are two schools of thought regarding how decisions get made in an interview. One school says that people make up their minds in the first five minutes. This approach is certainly questionable in its reliability, but you have to allow for it. So a firm handshake and a professional demeanor are important. The second school is more about using techniques such as behavioral interviewing to get a better sense of a candidate's true abilities. We will talk more about the behavioral interview in the next section, so for now, simply ensure that you manage the first impression in a favorable manner.

ADDRESS THE INTERVIEWER BY NAME; ASK FOR A BUSINESS CARD

If you can address interviewers by their title (Mrs., Ms., Dr., and so on) initially, then do so. If they tell you to call them by their first name, do so; but try to wait until they tell you to do so. It is presumptuous to refer to people by their first name, especially if they are hiring managers or others with seniority. It is better to err on the side of being conservative. Also, get a copy of their business card, and if they do not have one, ask them if you can write down their name and contact information. After you finish the interview, it is a good idea to send a brief thank-you note (preferably an e-mail, but you can also send a handwritten note). You will need their contact information in order to send the note.

DRESS PROFESSIONALLY

We already addressed this in the preparation portion, but be professional in everything you do. An entrepreneur who is working toward developing a new client wants to come across professionally. Again, it is the same for you. Think like an entrepreneur and be professional.

Remember, the purpose of the interview is to predict future job performance based on the applicant's oral responses to oral inquiries. The recruiter essentially wants to know if you can do the work, will you do the work, and will you fit in. Conversely, you want to know if you will be able to do the kind of work you want to do, if you will be able to draw on your past experiences in order to help you be successful, and if you will fit it. Both parties want to resolve the same questions, so be honest in your responses. If you wind up getting a job because you misrepresented an item in the interview and it is a job doing something you are not good at, both you and the employer will be dissatisfied. You are looking for a win-win situation. Which, it just so happens, is the same thing that an entrepreneur is trying to accomplish when selling his or her product or service. You want to arrive at a decision that is good for you and the employer.

SITUATIONAL AND BEHAVIORAL INTERVIEW QUESTIONS

During the interview you may get asked all sorts of things, but remember the key questions recruiters want answered:

1. Can you do the work?
2. Will you be able and motivated to do the work in their environment?
3. Will you fit in with their culture, value systems, and commitment to their customers and other external entities?

A key thing to remember is it is also important for you to resolve the same questions in your own mind. You do not want to get into a situation where you feel the need to change jobs three or four months after joining a firm. You may not work there for your entire career, but you want to have a shot at something that has some degree of longevity and professional development associated with it.

To help get at these concepts more reliably, recruiters employ a fairly common technique that uses either a situational or a behavioral questions.

SITUATIONAL QUESTIONS

When recruiters use this technique, they describe a hypothetical situation and then ask the candidate to describe how he or she would handle the situation. There is not a lot of preparation you can do for situational interviews, but remember the three key items of importance to any employer from chapter 7. They are:

1. People
2. Customers
3. Business

The reason you want to remember these three elements is that if you are asked a situational type question, you can answer it honestly and also try to include how you would effectively work with the people in the organization, pay close attention to serving the customer, and ensure that the profitability of the organization does not suffer.

The reality is that if you do not have a productive team, you will lose to the competition. If you do not maintain and build your customer base, you are out of business. And if your revenue is not greater than your expenses, you are out of business. When you decide how to respond to a situational question, keep these three mandates in mind and try to weave a response that maximizes one or more of them.

A possible situational question could be: "Suppose you realize that you will be late on a project. How would you handle it?"

Good responses would have an element of serving the customer, keeping the flow of communication going, and doing everything you can to have the best possible outcome. A bad response would be to simply accept the project is going to be late, keep it secret from management, or to do something that might have a detrimental impact on the customer.

One way to respond to a situational question is to utilize a leadership model that I have used from time to time. Essentially the model has four elements and are associated with the acronym VALUE. The elements are Vision—what you would like to achieve in response to the situational question. The second one is Alignment—how would you pull the resources together to achieve the desired response for the situational question. The third is Understanding—how would you communicate the desired outcome to the stakeholders and the fourth is Enactment—how would you make it happen.

Let me give you a brief example. Perhaps an interviewer would ask you a question such as: You are going to miss a deadline and you need to take action. What would you do? First, your Vision would be that you are going to do everything humanly possible not to miss the deadline. Your Alignment strategy would be to pull together all of the people available to help you, review their priorities and even make sure that you are working on the most critical components of the project that is in jeopardy of being late. You would generate understanding by not only telling your team what they would need to do but also ensure that the customer knows the status and what you are doing to meet the deadline. The fourth part of your response would be in terms of the enactment strategy. Explain what you are putting in place to ensure that the proper accountability and follow up strategies are in place.

By using the VALUE approach, you are responding to a situational question in the same vein as a leader in the organization would respond. It will go a long way in helping the employer see your potential as a key contributor to the organization's objectives.

Situational questions can actually be fairly easy to respond to because you get to use your imagination and describe a hypothetical situation. Just be sure to answer the question in a way that conveys you will make decisions and take actions that are good for the company, and not necessarily just good for you.

BEHAVIORAL QUESTIONS

A behavioral question has the intention of revealing how you actually behaved in the past when confronted with a given situation. It is based on the philosophy that the best predictor of future performance is past performance. The idea is that you can tell someone anything about how you might behave when you have to deal with a hypothetical tough customer, financial challenge, or uncooperative team member, but a behavioral question gets at how you actually did behave in the specific situation.

It is definitely possible for you to prepare for a behavioral question, and you should take the time to do so. Begin your preparation process by revisiting your personal value proposition. What are the key attributes you want someone to know about you? How can you operationalize them? As you think through them, identify four or five examples of behavior in your past that had outstanding results and that you would want to share with interviewers as examples of your focus on positive results. Pick some that talk about the customer, profitability, and organizational process improvement. Then, when you are asked a question, you can dip into your reserve of potential answers and give one that meets your needs and theirs.

For instance, a typical behavioral question would be something like: "Tell me a time when you had to deal with a tough customer."

If you have a great story about a tough customer that conveys a positive outcome in terms you believe are important to you and the company, go ahead and tell the story. If you do not have one about a tough customer, pick one about a tough professor or a tough coworker. The key is that if an interviewer asks you this question, he or she wants to know how you have behaved in the past when confronted by someone who was difficult. How did you deal with an individual who was a challenge?

One thing that I do want to emphasize here is that you want to make it compelling and interesting. In short, you want to tell a story, not just list a collection of activities that you did. As you prepare for the interview, practice telling the story about what happened and why someone would care about what you are saying. Interviewers want to connect with you on a personal level and if you tell them a compelling story, it is more likely that they will connect to who you are and want to know more about you.

Telling a compelling story is not easy. It takes practice but once you get good at it, the story will flow, and you will know that you are making a connection with the recruiter. Take some time, practice your story, maybe even read a little about the art of storytelling and then deliver your response to the question in a way that will make even the toughest recruiter want to know more about you and what you have done.

WHEN YOU INTERVIEW, YOU WANT TO BE A STAR

In crafting your response to a behavioral question, I recommend that you include the following four elements:

1. The **situation**
2. Your **task**(s) in that situation
3. The **action** that you took in response to the situation
4. The **results** that occurred as a direct result of your actions

Describe the **situation**. Be succinct and get to the point, but be sure to give the recruiter a sense of where you are and the overall environment.

When You Interview, You Want to Be a STAR

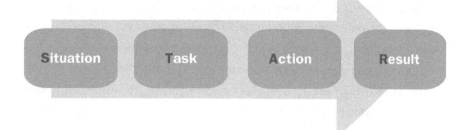

Situation | Task | Action | Result

FIGURE 11.1. ELEMENTS TO INCLUDE IN A SUCCESSFUL RESPONSE TO A BEHAVIORAL BASED QUESTION.

After that, describe the specific **task** that you were asked to perform. Did you have to respond to a specific irate customer, deal with a challenging employee, or maybe develop a cost-saving approach? Be specific. Make certain that the recruiter knows exactly what you were asked to do or what you chose to do on your own in the situation.

Thirdly, describe the **action** that you took. This is probably the longest part of the response. Describe what you did, what happened, and how it led to the outcome.

Be sure to include strong results directly tied to what you did!

And lastly, be sure to describe the **results**. What was the outcome? What happened as a result of your behavior that had a direct impact on the customer, the profitability of the firm, and/or the ongoing operational processes? Do not just let it die. This is where you drive home the outcome of your behavior and why it is important. You could describe a situation in which you dealt with an unhappy customer, but if it did not lead to anything positive, it will not be as impressive as if it led to action on behalf of a customer that was beneficial for the firm.

Some companies actually look for an additional item under the results section in terms of what you might have done differently if you had the chance to do it again. That is certainly an appropriate part of the response, so include it if it makes sense. In fact, don't be surprised if the recruiter uses it as a follow-up question. It is important to convey you are able to learn from every experience you have.

And, by the way, you want to do this in a response that takes from twenty seconds to two minutes. Twenty seconds is actually a long time in an interview, so practice some of your responses so you get a feel for how long you are taking.

A variation on this theme is to use the three letters *CAR*. *C* stands for "challenge," *A* for "action," and *R* for "results." In fact, some employers also add a *D* to that formula and, again, ask you to describe what you might do differently.

The key is that if you can use the idea of a challenge to introduce the situation and your resulting behavior, it can even be more impactful than using a routine example.

Use your own judgment in deciding which situations you want to describe, but those that convey a strong sense of overcoming a challenge will be perceived positively by a recruiter.

There are a couple more things to consider regarding behavioral questions. If interviewers ask you to give an example when something happened, give them an example and be specific. Do not answer in generalities. They want to know about a specific situation, so be sure to be specific.

Also, even if they do not ask you to tell them a specific example of something that happened, it might still be a behavioral question. For instance, if someone were to ask you who your role model is, the quick answer might be your father or mother, Martin Luther King, Jr., Mother Theresa, Jesus, Mohamed, or Presidents Bush or Obama. Those answers alone do not tell the recruiter anything. It is easy to say that a well-known figure is a role model.

It is important for you to then describe a specific behavior, using the STAR approach, of what you have done as a result of that person's influence in your life. The bottom line is that recruiters are looking for behaviors that are predictors of your success in their firm. And, again, as an entrepreneur you must be able to talk about what you have done that has been successful with a reasonable assumption that you would behave in a similar manner in the future. Always shoot for a win-win scenario.

As you get to the end of the interview, be sure to ask questions. One of the things to consider is that most recruiters are strongly committed to their company. Recruiting is a tough job; to go out every day and present your company to people, review resumes, and listen to interviews can be demanding. Recruiters are willing to do it because they believe in the company they represent. During the interview, you may feel they have answered all your questions, but if you do not have some to ask, you are essentially telling them you are not interested in their company. Remember, it is the company they are strongly committed to representing. Bad move! Not only does it convey that you have not done your homework, you can actually be offending the recruiters because of the commitment they have made to their company and their own careers.

Have some good questions to ask and don't make them about the dress code or the cafeteria. Make them about the business, the customer, what it takes to be successful, what challenges the company faces, and so on. Making your questions meaningful, relevant, and well thought out will greatly enhance your prospects for employment. Besides, an entrepreneur would want to learn all he or she could about a potential client. The same thing applies for you in your career search!

DIFFERENT LOCATIONS

In addition to the traditional interview format in a recruiter or hiring manager's office, there are also other forms of interviews such as telephone interviews, panel interviews or even ones in airports or hotel lobbies. Don't worry about the different formats. They are still after the same basic information. In fact, team interviews are often used to help the candidate gain a realistic job preview of what they can expect so that everyone is making a more informed decision. It helps you make a better decision along with them, so embrace the different formats that they may have in mind for you. They are all leading to the same desired outcome.

CLOSING THE DEAL

Well, you did it! You successfully developed your personal value proposition and a compelling personal story using a cover letter, a resume, and an engaging electronic portfolio. You prepared extensively for the interview and were able to clearly articulate how you would handle a myriad of challenges if they came your way. The recruiters are impressed. They have passed you on to the hiring manager, and she has finished her assessment of your abilities. You both believe you are in a win-win situation and are anxious to come to agreement about compensation and get the paperwork signed.

SALARY NEGOTIATION

What do you do? More specifically, what do you do regarding compensation nego-tiation? Accept what they offer? Tell them you want more regardless of the offer?

One more time, you want to approach this situation just like an entrepreneur. You want to be sure you receive appropriate compensation for the value you will bring to the firm.

People ask for money because they want it, they need, it or they deserve it. The third reason is the only one that is relevant.

When people approach the whole idea of getting a salary offer—or asking for a raise, a better grade in school, or a promotion at work—they are generally driven by three different levels of motivation. Simply stated, they feel they want it, they need it, or they deserve it.

The argument for wanting it is generally based on what you feel other people may be getting, but this is generally not defensible since it is based more on your personal sense of equity and not on facts. We all want more. So what? Just because you want it is not a reason to justify a certain level of compensation.

The second argument is based on need. I need it because I just bought a new car, I just got married, or I have a new child. This type of reason can be emotional and can drive people to be pretty aggressive with their requests, but again it is not a reason to justify any level of compensation. Your needs are a result of choices you have made, and although they can play into the compensation equation, they really cannot support an argument for a given compensation package.

The only argument that will hold water is that you deserve it. You need to do your homework. Research compensation levels for your area and the job you are going into. Be reasonable with your request. Let the data support you.

When you do your research you may get a specific value or a range. If you get the specific value, you should create some kind of range to go with it. Ranges vary from 30 percent to 50 percent of the spread, so a 50 percent range on a $50,000 midpoint would be 25 percent in each direction, or from $37,500 to $62,500. As you can see, a 50 percent range is quite broad; most ranges will be more in the 30 percent to 40 percent range. If you are calculating your own range from a midpoint you identified from your research, I recommend that you use the 40 percent figure unless you know it to be different.

Once you have a range, and if you are just getting started in the field, it would be appropriate to request something in the midpart of the lower end of the range. Conversely, if you have several years of experience, requesting something in the midpart of the higher end of the range would not be out of reason.

The key is that you want to do your research, be reasonable, be respectful, give them a range to work with, and above all else, base it on objective data.

Also, realize that even if you have the ranges for a given job, you will need to get a feel for the individual company's compensation philosophy. Do they actually pay for performance, or just claim that they do? Do they have an annual raise structure with limited flexibility, or can people get raises at any time during the year? Are they choosing to meet the market, or lead it, or even potentially lag the current market values? For instance, if the position has a lot of potential candidates, it is likely that the company will be choosing to meet or even lag the market but if there are only a few potential candidates, some companies will choose to lead the market.

The key is that you want to be informed so do your research but also ask questions in the recruiting process that indicate that you understand the basics of corporate compensation and want to ensure that there is a good match between the company's philosophy and your own sense of expectations.

Lastly, be sure to consider the benefits package in calculating your total compensation. Benefits can often be 30 percent of base compensation or even higher for some positions. Also, there may be the opportunity for bonuses, so be sure to take everything into consideration. Most salary surveys are calculated based on base salary, so you will probably have to do your own extrapolation for bonuses and benefits—but they all factor into the equation.

Good luck, and have some fun with the process. You have done a great job preparing for the process and you deserve to be happy, proud of what you have done, and excited about the world of possibilities that is opening up for you.

AFTER THE INTERVIEW

Finally, when you finish the interview be sure to send a thank-you note. I recommend you send one via e-mail before the end of the day. Some people recommend a handwritten note; for more senior positions, that might be appropriate, but for most positions, recruiters will be back at the hotel or office reading e-mails, and when they get a message from you, it can leave a favorable impression with them. Needless to say, be sure it is grammatically flawless. Read it closely. Consider reading it backward. It does not need to be long. Simply tell the recruiter you enjoyed meeting with him or her, you feel you can be a valuable addition to the firm, and you look forward to continuing the dialog about this opportunity.

Not to belay the point too much, but it is definitely what an entrepreneur would do after he or she has made an initial pitch to a potential customer. Do not rely on the recruiter to take all the initiative. You need to do some yourself, and it starts with a prompt, error-free thank-you note. (If there is more than one interviewer, send a note addressed to each of them separately.)

There is no one best way to follow up while you wait to hear from recruiters. In fact, there are many situations in which recruiters will want to keep you active in the process even if they are not yet ready to give you the offer. They may have other candidates to interview, or they may need to pursue further hiring approval, so be patient. You should not contact them every day, but it does not hurt to follow up every week or so to see how things are proceeding. It is fine to check, and it tells the recruiter that you are still interested.

Follow up in a professional manner, and if you get an offer, be prepared to evaluate and accept it within a few days if you are so inclined. A word to the wise. Every offer has three elements:

1. The start date
2. The compensation
3. The job title

Anything else is simply a statement of interest. When you receive a job offer with these three elements, then the ball is in your court to accept, negotiate, or decline. However, until you receive an offer, you are just in the mode of having a dialog, so if you have other options, continue to pursue them at the same time.

ADDITIONAL RESOURCES

Like most other subjects related to career planning and development, they are a multitude of resources on the internet that can help you. If you are a student, or even a recent alumnus, you might want to contact your university's career services department or the alumni office for access to tools that may be of value. Some schools have an agreement with a company called **Big Interview** while others might be connected to a package called **Optimal Resume**. If you have access to either of these resources, be sure to take advantage of them. They can provide you with a wealth of practice opportunities before you get into your real interview.

Another option is to see if your career center can arrange for a mock Interview for you to practice. Many schools also have this option available and if yours does, take advantage of it.

Monster.com and Glassdoor.com also have resources that can help you with your interviewing and don't forget to simply do a Google search and find the most current information about interviewing as well as more resources to help you in the process.

You can also learn more about the idea of story telling especially when it comes to the use of technology to help in the process. The following website is about the use of artificial intelligence in the development of a compelling story. Check it out and then read more about the whole idea of telling stories in a compelling manner.

https://www.fastcompany.com/3067836/robot-revolution/why-google-ideo-and-ibm-are-betting-on-ai-to-make-us-better-storytellers?utm_source=mailchimp&utm_medium=email&utm_campaign=fast-company-daily-newsletter&position=intro&partner=newsletter&campaign_date=02062017

Good luck in your quest.

NOW WHAT?

The best way to improve your oral communication skills is to practice with real people in real settings. However, it can be intimidating the first time, so if you have any trepidation, do a little practice at home in a safe setting. Here are some suggestions:

1. Write down your elevator speech and then practice saying it in front of a mirror until it flows naturally. You do not want to sound like you are reciting something from memory, even though you are. Try to make it sound spontaneous and interesting, but be sure to cover the main points.

2. Think about creating your own logo or visual image to help guide you in the process. Maybe something as simple as a box with three lines enclosed in a circle would work for you. You could say it stands for strength of character in the face of adversity while still maintaining a global perspective, or something like that. I am obviously making this one up. But I use the triangle we discussed in the book on my business cards to help lead the conversation when I introduce myself. You can certainly do the same thing.

3. Speaking of business cards, get some and practice handing them out when you meet someone.

4. Regarding interviews, try to do some mock interviews if your college's career center will set them up. If not, you might be able to work with a student organization to invite recruiters to come to campus to do mock interviews. Do not wait until you have the real one lined up for it to be your first.

5. One option to practice interviewing beyond mock interviews is to investigate some of the software available through your career center. Optimal Resume is one such package; it has the option to record and play back your answers to questions and can be a great resource to help you practice.

6. And lastly, commit to one or two specific things that you can do to help improve your interviewing skills. Add it to your career plan and then follow up and make it happen.

The key is to practice. First, do it in a safe environment and maybe even get some of your friends to work with you, and then get out and do some networking. Set an objective to go to some kind of networking event on a regular basis and then follow through. The people who develop strong networking skills and are able to talk about their abilities are the ones who get the opportunities.

You might look great on paper, but it is the personal contact that closes the deal. And you must practice the personal contact in order to become a master. Make the commitment to take the required time, invest in yourself, and reap the rewards.

Good luck!

SECTION FIVE.

MAKING IT HAPPEN

INTRODUCTION

After you have done all the preparatory work and developed a compelling personal value proposition that is in line with your skills and abilities, you must actually make something happen. So far, this has been an interesting experience. You have learned how to think more like an entrepreneur, how to get over the rough spots, and how to understand yourself better. You now know what your personal brand is, how to look for potential under-served needs, and how to articulate your personal value proposition in response to those needs. And lastly, you have learned how to tell your story better through written media, oral communication, and use of the internet and social media.

But now it all comes down to making something happen. This next section will help you pull together what you will need for a comprehensive personal career-acceleration plan that will serve you in the months and years to come. Take the time to build your plan, find a mentor, explore the potential opportunities that exist, and make it all work for you!

Good luck in your endeavor.

12

Developing and Executing Your Personal Career-Acceleration Plan

SUMMARY OF THE COMPONENTS

As a reminder, here is a summary of the nine components that can go into the development of your personal career-acceleration plan.

SELF-ASSESSMENT

Be honest with yourself and be critical of your skills and abilities. Take a good hard look at what you can do and where you need to grow. Be candid about your career dilemma. Share it with people whom you trust. Be explicit and honest with yourself. Conduct a SWOT analysis of your personal situation. Keep this information on hand. Periodically review it and update it as you make progress toward your goals.

Do not be overly critical, but do be honest and establish where you currently stand. Be sure to keep track of your progress and update your records accordingly. Celebrate the successes, and reward yourself when you do make progress.

ENTREPRENEURIAL MIND-SET

This is what will make all of the difference in your career pursuits, and it all starts with the simple idea of learning to think like an entrepreneur. Look around at people who are pursuing successful careers and think about the things that make them successful. Accept the fact that you must be competitive in a global marketplace—but this competition provides you with innumerable opportunities. Accept the fact that you are a company of one and you are an entrepreneur of your own skills and abilities. Then you are ready to proceed with the next step in the process.

SURVIVE, ADAPT, AND FLOURISH

Career planning is a process, not an event. It may have many different iterations, and you will be developing and launching many goals and objectives throughout your career. Use this template to help keep things in perspective and to keep you going forward.

Survive: Understand what you need to accomplish in order to take care of the basic necessities. It might be your financial needs or even more fundamental needs pertaining to your personal well-being. Identify what they are and what must to do in order to gain them.

Adapt: Strive to be open to the potential opportunities that surround you every day. Do not discard an idea just because it is strange or you have not done it before. It may even be something you feel can be done better by someone else. Identify these potential opportunities, and for those that most interest you, identify the personal strategy you must follow in order to make them a reality.

Flourish: Identify your long-term goals and keep your focus on achieving them. Measure your progress toward them on a regular basis. Stay on course and adjust your strategy when necessary. Above all else, don't forget to have some fun along the way.

PERSONAL BRANDING

In order to compete in today's economy, you must develop a personal brand and a subsequent marketing strategy to get your brand out in the marketplace. It may be a few key words, or maybe even a symbol that captures the essence of what you do and the value you bring. Think about some of the more successful brands in today's business climate and seek to develop your brand with the same level of excitement, uniqueness, and value that will encourage others to want to associate with you.

PERSONAL VALUE PROPOSITION

If you are selling something as an entrepreneur, you must be able to describe what you have to offer in terms understood by the buyer. Develop your personal value proposition with a view toward the value that you bring to the marketplace. As you develop your personal value proposition, you will develop not only a strong sense of your value but also the self-confidence that comes with having something of true value. Keep it brief enough so that you can share it with others, but above all else, ensure that it is responsive to the market and not simply serving your personal needs. By developing and understanding the resulting sweet spot—where your brand, the under-served need, and your personal value proposition come together—you will be bulletproof today and well into the future.

FINDING THE UNDER-SERVED NEED

As we have said throughout the book, this process is not a completely linear one. As you develop one area, you may need to double back and redo some of the work you did in a previous section. That said, you need to identify where you can best apply your abilities. This under-served need will have two components. It will be an area in which you have a unique interest and in which there is a unique demand. Try not to settle for just one. Set your goals to achieve both, and in your quest strive to identify the needs that require being served but are also in tune with your areas of interest.

TELLING YOUR STORY

WRITTEN MEDIA

Resume

Your resume should be one page if possible, two at the most. It must be flawless in terms of both spelling and grammar and able to be read in twenty seconds. It should give readers a clear sense of your personal value proposition and how you can bring value to their specific company. There are numerous formats and choices for you to use. However, do not believe that a resume will do your job search for you. It can serve you, but you must decide how it is going to do so and then design it accordingly.

Cover Letter

Your cover letter should have three sections: an *introduction*, which should include the job title for which you are applying; the *body*, which should be closely aligned with your personal value proposition and also delineate how you can provide value to the specific job requirements; and the *close*, in which you take responsibility for the next steps as much as is possible. Again, it has to be flawless as well as professional and respectful.

SOCIAL MEDIA

Facebook, Twitter, LinkedIn, and Electronic Portfolios

Clean up Facebook, tap into the resources on Twitter, sign in to LinkedIn, and decide how you want your presence to exist in the electronic media. You may want to create your own electronic portfolio or web page or engage in blogs and other means of communication. The key is to make it purposeful. Use these tools to serve your needs and do not allow them to be created simply because you have chosen to use one over the other. Take the time to develop your strategy and then periodically review what you are actually doing against that strategy.

ORAL MEDIA

Networking

Look for opportunities to meet other people. Get your business cards ready, along with your personal value proposition and elevator speech. Look for opportunities to serve others. Remember, networking is as much about giving as it is about getting. When you meet others, ask them what they do for a living and look for opportunities to help them. Start your personal networking by focusing more on giving. The getting will come along in its own time, and it will be significant when it does come.

Interviewing

If you know your brand and your personal value proposition and have researched the company to gain a strong understanding of the under-served need, then interviewing becomes much more like a dance than a test. You are looking for a match between you and the company, so be able to talk about the value you bring. Remember the STAR approach for those behavioral questions. Practice whenever you get the chance. Cherish any feedback you get from employers, but always stay focused on the value you bring to them and how you can help them be more successful.

PERSONALIZE YOUR PLAN

All of this will only work if you are able to take the concepts, internalize them, understand where you stand on each of them, and ultimately develop a plan to help you grow in each of the areas. The first three areas discussed in the book are all about exploring your passion and will help you understand yourself better. The next three are about discovering the opportunities and are focused on the market. The final three help you tell your story more effectively.

It would be nice if life were a linear process, and we could get from point A to point Z by simply following the twenty-four steps in-between. However, life is very messy, and so there will be setbacks that require reworking ideas and changing and adjusting objectives along the way. However, do not let that stop you from developing a plan. My recommendation to you is to start small. Identify one or two ways that you can improve in each of the nine areas outlined in the book. Set some tangible, realistic goals with clear deliverables and target dates and then hold yourself accountable to achieving them. If you fail, take a look at what happened, adjust the goal, and do it again.

RINSE AND REPEAT

Your career-planning process is recursive and will continue for the rest of your professional life. We use the idea of rinse and repeat to summarize that idea. You are never fully finished and are constantly a work in progress. But by pursuing this approach, you will be more likely to find a career that challenges and engages you while also doing something that you enjoy.

One more thing to consider: try to find yourself a mentor. It is great to have someone in your professional life who can give you feedback and advice going forward. Take the time to find the right mentor. Share your approach with that person, and if you can find someone who is supportive, understands what you are trying to accomplish, and is committed to being there for you, you will be successful.

ADDITIONAL RESOURCES

In addition to the resources we included in chapters 3 and 7, here are some further resources for you to pursue.

Comb the local press (newspapers and magazines) for formal networking events. Informal networking can also take place at an array of other events such as:

- Public lectures at your local library college / university
- Trade shows
- Book signings
- Chamber of Commerce meetings
- Economic Club meetings
- Civic clubs
- Charitable events
- Conferences

Detroit News Business Section,
  http://www.detroitnews.com/business/
  (Sign up for the free e-newsletter)

Detroit Free Press, Weekly Business Calendar,
http://www.freep.com/story/money/business
/2015/04/26/business-calendar/26271983/

Crain's Detroit Business Calendar of Events,
http://www.crainsdetroit.com/section/events

Identify key researchers in your subject field by periodically checking conference literature. Take advantage of the free databases available through the Michigan Electronic Library (MeL). Begin at your local public library's website and look for the MeL link. Choose the Academic OneFile database. Limit your search to one of these categories:

- Conference News
- Conference Notes
- Conference Overview

In addition to this content, if you are a student within the University of Michigan system, here are some additional resources you can access through the Mardigian Library:

Take advantage of lectures and events taking place at UM Dearborn, especially when the speakers or sponsors are from a company or industry of interest.

Join the student chapter of relevant professional organizations (American Marketing Association, etc.) and participate fully.

To locate Michigan associations, use the print book, *Michigan Associations Directory*. It can be checked out even though it is a reference book.

AS28.M5 M53 1997, Reference/1st Floor
Mardigian Library

To locate key researchers or thought leaders in your subject area, use the **Web of Science** database available through the Mardigian Library. Limit your search to

"Conference Proceedings Citation Index" then type a search term in the search box (i.e. digital marketing).

[OR]

In the ABI/INFORM database, limit your search to "Conference Papers & Proceedings."

NOW WHAT?

So much potential and so little time. It can truly be overwhelming but if you want to truly be empowered and successful in your career quest, it is important that you do the work to help prepare you for the main round. So, begin at the beginning. Take the time to reflect on what you have read. Make the commitment to understand what it takes to think like an entrepreneur. Meet with people who have a clear entrepreneurial mind-set. Read something about the idea. Practice playing with the idea when you talk with other people. You will quickly receive the sense from them that you are on the right path. Listen to that feedback and continue to build your sense of being I Inc.

Look at the other sections and decide what you can do to make them part of your professional career aspirations. If you take the time to explore many of the suggestions in the "Now What?" sections at the end of each chapter, you will be well on your way to the development and implementation of a successful career quest.

CONCLUSION

If this book is going to be of service to you, it must help you create a context for success and then guide you through an ongoing process to exploit that context.

Successful entrepreneurs survey the market, launch a business enterprise, succeed or fail, and do it again. They are constantly adjusting the value proposition they bring to the market. It is both the reality and the beauty of a capitalistic system that has provided the world with the highest standard of living possible.

Embrace it and use it to serve your purposes. There will always be challenges as well as change in the system. However, do not lose faith in the process. It has served millions of entrepreneurs as they have built successful businesses, and it can serve you by providing you with a career development process that will serve you for your entire professional career.

This book is all about capturing this context and helping you, the job seeker, apply those concepts in a way that enables you to participate in the abundance that can exist in your life.

Take the time to embrace these concepts. Do a critical analysis of your abilities, scan the market, look for the under-served need,and then prepare to bring your ability to the market to meet that need.

Conceptually, it is quite simple, but its application will require time, dedication, and an unwavering focus on the outcome. Use a checklist to remind you of where you are and what you need to do. Keep track of your progress. Above all else, have faith in the free enterprise system and your ability to participate successfully in it. Your career will bloom and continue to grow throughout your professional life. Give it a chance. You have everything to gain and nothing to lose.

Good luck and have some fun. You deserve it!

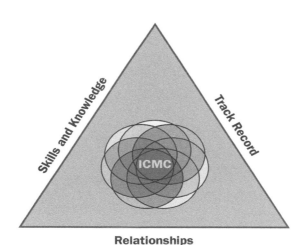

Relationships
Internship and Career Management Center

FIGURE 12.1. TRIANGLE OF SUCCESS.
Copyright © by Internship & Career Management Center, University of Michigan-Dearborn. Reprinted with permission.

INDEX